Praise from readers for *Connecting:*

"A delightful, practical, and spiritually stimulating guide to making contact with that true self within."—Dr. Donald Curtis, radio talk-show host

"I found myself pausing and instantly connecting a person in my life with an example of behavior the author was describing, and then I made a connection with the wisdom of her words. This book has helped me call on my higher self. I know I will use it as a resource manual."—Mark Dietz, President, Concord Realty, an international real estate investment firm

"A major part of my job is to help people deal more compassionately with people who report to them. *Connecting* will be extremely useful in that area. The practical format of short, meaty chapters fits the way most businesspeople work. I intend to use this book as a training tool. In addition to individual development, it has valuable information on methods of building a cooperative work environment."—Kate Ludeman, Director of Human Resources for KLA Instruments, a Silicon Valley firm

"I am feeling a curious blend of excitement and peace. The excitement comes from the thought that these concepts of aliveness are going to reach the world in a form that is so useful and practical. The peace comes from my own personal experience reading the book and acting on it right now. While reading, I felt the poetry of the author's words and thoughts caress me and soothe burdens large and small."—Linda Johnston, M.D., Van Nuys, California

CONNECTING

CONNECTING

With All the People in Your Life

64 Ways to Open Communications & Enrich Your Relationships

LaUna HUFFINES

1817

Harper & Row, Publishers, San Francisco

Cambridge, Hagerstown, New York, Philadelphia
London, Mexico City, São Paulo, Singapore, Sydney

FIRST EDITION

Library of Congress Cataloging-in-Publication Data

Huffines, LaUna.
  Connecting with all the people in your life.

    1. Interpersonal relations—Problems, exercises, etc.
  2. Interpersonal relations—Miscellanea.
  3. Interpersonal communication—Problems, exercises, etc.
  4. Interpersonal communications—Miscellanea.
  I. Title.
HM132.H83   1986   302.3'4   85-45716
ISBN 0-06-250400-2

86 87 88 89 90 HC 10 9 8 7 6 5 4 3 2 1

I dedicate this book to the awakening nobility
within all people,
which offers joy and purpose,
harmony and love,
compassion and truth,
and recognizes an equal nobility in others.

Contents

Acknowledgments

In heartfelt gratitude and acknowledgment to:

Sanaya Roman and Orin, who inspired me with their friendship, encouragement, and many suggestions.

Craig Comstock, who helped me with the early development of the book and assisted in planning the format.

Elaine Ratner, who loyally joined me in a two-month marathon of editing and revising to make each chapter more practical and succinct.

Linda Mead, who has energetically and skillfully guided the marketing of this book.

John Loudon, Clayton Carlson, Mike Kehoe, Tom Dorsaneo, and Brian Erwin, whose combined editing, publishing, and marketing talents made the publication of this book a delight.

John Enright, my teaching partner for seven years, with whom many of these "beyond" concepts were co-created, researched, and developed.

My four sons, Phillip, Donald, Ray, and James, whose relationships to me and to each other as they grew up stimulated the birth of many of these ideas.

Roberto Assagioli, whose manuscripts, published and unpublished, inspired my work on connecting our inner qualities with our outer lives.

Leslie Bandler, Richard Bandler, and Robert Dilts, whose thorough training techniques in Neuro-Linguistic Programming strongly influenced this book.

Some of the early readers who gave practical, intuitive, or technical support during the years of writing this manuscript:

Robert Muller, Laura Huxley, Larry Dossey, M.D., Ken Wilber, Richard Ryal, Linda Johnston, M.D., Kate Ludeman, Phillip Zimbardo, Angeles Arrien, Peter Caddy, Piero Ferrucci, David and Donna Chamberlain, Rev. Donald Curtis, Gov. William P. Clements, Jr., Duane Packer, Jean St. Martin, Sam and Wren Caudle, Cissy Howell, Paul Herman, Amerinda and Ed Alpern, Jane Schaefer Huffines, Patricia and Mark Dietz, Gloria Buller, Pat McCartney, E. M. Bush, Rev. James

Hempstead, Jim Bolen, Frances Vaughan, Roger Walsh, Orest Bedrij, Marie Hagelstein, Susan Horton, Rob Roman, Bob DuBerry, Rev. LeRoy Zemke, Vishwanath Naravane, Eve Weir Curtis, Teresa Colleton, James Dixon, Jeff Abbott, Meg O'Brien, Janet Reed, Pat LaForce, and Barbara Edelston.

The Way In

All of us are limited in our relationships by boundaries we drew at some time in the past. In effect, we drew a line that said, "You can come this far, but no closer." Or, "You've treated me thoughtlessly and I'm going to treat you thoughtlessly too." We may have set up these boundaries long ago to protect ourselves from getting hurt. But, sooner or later, the limits that have protected us will also isolate us from making deeply satisfying relationships—from really *connecting*. Fortunately, if we've put up fences, we can learn to cut gates in them; if we have built walls, we can add doorways. Through these openings we will find the way in.

All our relationships are woven together to form the tapestry of our lives. Each person we truly care about is a new color, a different design, or an interesting texture for us to add. At times we may weave uneven patterns, or use dull colors. When we think of the imperfect ways in which we communicate with our parents, our life partners, our children, friends, and coworkers, we sense that our designs might be brighter and richer. As long as we live we will create more patterns, pick up forgotten threads, and weave them in to make new connections.

When we really *connect* with another person—or even with ourselves—we are enriched by the relationship. In this book you will learn how to form new connections in which you feel truly loved and understood. You will learn to transform any unsatisfying relationships into joyous and enriching ones. This book offers you new, pure colors to choose from, different patterns to weave; you will learn how to unravel patterns that are already set, and to reweave them according to your new vision of who you are.

A gifted psychologist once told me that what amazed him the most, after years of helping clients, was how little most people ask for. I have written this book for everyone who wants more, who seeks to create deeply satisfying connections and to enjoy the vitality they bring to our lives.

WHAT IS A TRUE CONNECTION?

Connections do not happen by accident or fate, but neither do they take hard work or a long time to develop. To make a real connection with another person, you simply form a clear vision of the relationship you want and take concrete steps to create it.

What is a *true* connection? If you feel drained, obligated, or possessed by another person, you're missing a true connection. When you really connect, you'll know it immediately. Have you ever been with someone who recognizes and appreciates your innate value, yet asks nothing from you save to enjoy the pleasure of your company? The feeling of mutual appreciation, of caring and compassion, indicates a true connection.

Think of a moment in your childhood when you experienced an almost indescribable feeling of joy at your own energy and aliveness, or were overwhelmed with wonder at the power of the ocean or the vastness of the universe. Think of the warmth you received from a special friendship, or a moment in which you were so close to another person that you needed no words to communicate. Perhaps you can even remember a time when you were so quiet that you could hear the voice of your own intuition. This book will show you how to translate those feelings and experiences into a new approach to your relationships that you can put to use immediately.

It is only through making real connections that you discover your innate qualities and attain a larger sense of who you are. Two kinds of connections—with others and with yourself—can help you to experience more clearly your own beauty, compassion, and power. In the first, you see your own qualities reflected in someone else, almost as if the other person were a mirror. You can learn how to see your own higher qualities many times each day—not only in your intimate and enduring relationships, but in the eyes of a child, the smile of the checker at the supermarket, the voice of a waiter, the sound of a companion's laughter, or the words of a stranger.

The second kind of connection—with your self—is the source of your delight and fulfillment with others. You can discover your inner self by sitting alone in silence and becoming clearer about what you truly desire in your life and your relationships. As you gain better access to your own source of wisdom and compassion, you will gradually come to identify with your inner self, and stop being tossed about by the many sides of your personality that come into play throughout the day.

MEETING ALL THE SIDES OF YOURSELF AND FINDING YOUR TRUE SELF

We have all experienced the feeling that there is more than one of us running around in our bodies. If it's a beautiful summer day, our child self may want to play, while our critical self says that we will be in big trouble if we don't go back to work. If we ask our wise, inner consultant —our true self—we may decide to go to work, but also to enjoy a delightful lunch hour basking in the sun. Your inner consultant or true self is your wise and confident side, beckoning you to open new territory and to enrich your connections. This consultant has always whispered softly in your ear, yet its voice has almost always been drowned out by the noise of others or by your own mind.

In this book you learn to recognize and relate to all the selves within you with respect. All the parts of you want to help in some way, but they sometimes need more information on how best to do it. At times they seem like actors who are inventing their own scripts as they go along, without a sense of the overall plot or purpose of the play. Your true self knows how to direct the drama of your life and how to teach each actor to play new and far more effective roles.

Many names have been used to describe this self—the higher self, the true self, the inner self. Every religion uses different names and suggests different ways to make this connection. The only universal requirement is the will to know this part of yourself. There is no one right way to search. To find your true self, first acknowledge that you want a new sphere of companionship. Then set up a regular time and place to be with this self and *assume* that you have the companionship you seek, *even if you can see or hear nothing unusual.*

Just quieting your mind and emotions will allow you access to a different stream of knowing and seeing than you are used to.

If you have been taught that nothing comes except through effort, the ease of opening yourself may surprise you. The process is so simple that you may think you are making it all up. But if you are relaxed and willing to receive, you will be able to clear the static of daily life and tune into the channel that your true self uses to communicate with you.

HOW TO USE THIS BOOK

This book is designed to be read slowly, a chapter a day at the most. If you wish to read the book straight through to get an overall sense of its spirit, do so. But to derive full benefit, concentrate on one chapter each day, or even one a week. Absorb the material and take the suggested steps. New ways of seeing and acting that at first require conscious attention will soon become part of your everyday life.

This book is arranged in eight sections to take you through a natural progression. In the first two sections, you will practice opening, expanding, centering, and integrating to prepare you for acting from intention. The next three sections guide you through speaking and listening with integrity, enjoying freedom and abundance, and connecting with compassion. The last two sections explain how you can learn to trust your true self and honor the true self of others. Each chapter title is in two parts. First is the separating trait, the actions we take that limit us in our relationships (e.g., Beyond Holding a Fixed Position). This is followed by the connecting trait, which enables us to make true connections with the people in our lives (e.g., Increasing Flexibility).

You can read this book section by section, or read the chapters in any order. You may wish to look up a chapter that has special significance for you right now.

Although a great deal of research and counseling experience lies behind the information in this book, I have not cluttered the text with academic references or quotations. I invite you to look to your own authority, rather than to outside experts. The validity of the ideas in this book exists not in what someone else might have said, but in how you apply these principles to your own life. When a suggestion rings true, your own wisdom has been tapped. Listen to your inner self.

HOW TO DO THE EXERCISES

Each chapter calls upon memories of your attributes—many long-unused and forgotten—as well as your creative imagination for the future. The chapters encourage you to take your fears by the hand, as if they were a little brother or sister, and lead them to your new vision. The steps at the end of each chapter are carefully laid out so you can complete them in a few minutes. They offer you practice in applying the ideas you have just read. At the same time they assist you to expand your vision, to recall an inner loving wisdom, and to express this wisdom in each relationship. Prepare yourself to receive the full benefit of the exercises by sitting quietly for a few minutes and allowing yourself to relax fully before you begin. Your receptivity opens the door to discovery.

As you go through the steps, you may occasionally feel uncomfortable or resistant. Don't be discouraged. This feeling will be temporary and does not imply a lack of awareness on your part. Discomfort is often the step just before success. Remember that you are unraveling the patterns of a lifetime. Have faith in your vision of how much is possible and in the spirit of this book, and you will keep moving forward.

As you read and practice the exercises at the end of each chapter,* you may want to capture your own wisdom by writing your insights in a notebook. If so, include your new vision of what is possible, the actions you take, and the results you get. In this way you can see clearly the new patterns you are creating. What looks like change to others will seem to you like the natural way to see and do things.

Every now and then you will be challenged by an idea or step that seems more difficult. The promised apple may seem to be hanging from too high a branch. But as soon as you stretch a little for it, you will be nourished by fruit well worth the effort—and you will be surprised to find how far you can reach.

---

*An audio cassette tape is available to help you to open to deeper connections in your life. For information: Choosing Light, Inc., Box 5019, Mill Valley, California, 94942.

This is your way in. Now you are ready to begin your journey, starting tomorrow with Chapter 1. Make an appointment with yourself for just 15 uninterrupted minutes, free of whatever might otherwise distract you—television, the phone, business pressures, the children, errands, or even friends. Let this be your time, each day, in which to open to new levels of joy and delight in your connections with all the people in your life—including yourself.

How to Use the "Take Action" Cards

The cards provided with this book* offer you and the people in your life a way to create new relationships that are both fun and rewarding. You can use the cards by yourself, or play with others, in games that will lead to new insights.

Each card relates to a particular chapter. Here's how the cards are set up:

- Line 1: section name (e.g., Opening and Expanding)
- Line 2: chapter number (1 through 64)
- Line 3: separating trait (e.g., Beyond Present Boundaries)
- Line 4: connecting trait (e.g., Opening New Territory)

TO OPEN COMMUNICATION

Spread the cards face down and think of a specific person with whom you would like to have more open communication. Draw 1 card. Read the designated chapter and do the exercises, keeping that person in mind. To clarify how to begin using the connecting trait (line 4), draw a second card and proceed as above. Continue choosing cards until you feel confident that you understand the steps you will take. Then select a time and place to put your new knowledge into action.

TO ENRICH YOUR RELATIONSHIPS

Two people can use the cards to enrich their relationship. Players each select 3 cards that best represent the new connecting traits (line 4) they see developing in their partner. Each player in turn presents the cards to the other, one at a time, citing specific situations in which the partner went beyond the separating trait (line 3) and expressed the connecting

*The cards are located following chapter 52, page 131. Separate them at the perforations to form a deck. For information about obtaining additional sets of cards, write: Choosing Light, Inc., Box 5019, Mill Valley, California, 94942.

one. Expect to be surprised during the next week as you spontaneously give and receive on these new levels.

This game can also be played with a group of people. It is provocative and can stimulate thoughtful exchanges at dinner parties, family evenings, or group meetings. Deal out 12 cards to each person. (For more than 5 players, deal 6 to 8 cards each.) One person sits in the center. Each player selects from his or her cards the connecting trait (line 4) that he or she appreciates most about the person in the center, and then gives that card to the person. Each player takes a turn sitting in the center.

TO BREAK THROUGH OLD PATTERNS OF REACTING

Select the section of the book that relates to the area you want to change (e.g., Speaking and Listening with Integrity), and use only the 8 cards from that section. Or decide on a specific challenge before drawing. For example, if you want to develop a greater ability to enjoy freedom and abundance in your relationships, use only the cards numbered 33 to 40. Draw 1 card from your pile each morning, read the designated chapter and steps, and apply them with *each* person you meet that day—using an appropriate form of speech and action.

TO REDIRECT THE VARIOUS SIDES OF YOUR PERSONALITY

Begin by selecting a card that represents a separating trait (line 3) of a facet of your personality (e.g., "Beyond Holding a Fixed Position" for your stubborn self). Focus on the connecting quality (line 4) (e.g., "Increasing Flexibility"), and imagine how that part of you could speak and act with the wisdom of that trait.

TO CONNECT WITH JOYFUL PEOPLE

Select one connecting trait (line 4) that gives you the highest joy when you read it. Put the card on your mirror (or by your refrigerator, in your billfold, or any place you habitually look each day). When you look in your mirror each morning and see the card, imagine your day enriched by joyful discoveries and connections.

Gather books, music, poetry, pictures—all the things that give you a new feeling of joyous vitality.

Note in your journal the joyful moments that arise each day, and describe your ability to tap into joyous and harmonious feelings.

TO CONNECT WITH YOUR INTUITIVE WISDOM

Draw 1 card each day from Part VII, Trusting Your True Self, and read the designated chapter. Set aside quiet time alone to listen to your intuitive knowledge. (Allow 3 or 4 minutes to receive all you can use for the day—and 20 or 30 minutes for the mind to become quiet enough to let it in.)

TO HEAL PAST PAIN IN RELATING

With 2 or more players, state in a few brief sentences the outcome of a relationship in which you were hurt or felt pain. Choose the card that expresses the connecting trait (line 4) that would have created a different outcome—if it had been available to you. Read the corresponding chapter and then tell the same story again—this time acting as if you were a wise, compassionate person who easily expressed that connecting trait. Begin the story with your first inkling that things were going wrong, and tell what you would have said and done with the assistance of the connecting trait. Tell your story so well—even if you have to begin again several times—that your friends are convinced it could be true. This is a game of creative imagination that will alter the pain of the past and open you to an alternative—and far more enjoyable—future.

TO CONNECT IN A BUSINESS SETTING

Concentrate on your next business meeting—with a buyer, employee, client, patient, boss, coworker. Draw 1 to 3 cards from the deck. Then read the corresponding chapters and steps. Reflect on how you could express the connecting trait (line 4) in the meeting—how you would feel if you had it, how you would enter the room, what you would say. Run the scene through your mind, refining and polishing your words and actions until you are confident that you will make a good connection.

CONNECTING: 64 Ways to Enrich

OPENING AND EXPANDING	CENTERING AND INTEGRATING	ACTING FROM INTENTION	SPEAKING AND LISTENING WITH INTEGRITY
1 Beyond present boundaries Opening new territory	**9** Beyond withdrawing Finding your true center	**17** Beyond spending time together Choosing to connect	**25** Beyond feeling shy or hesitant Enjoying self-expression
2 Beyond practicality Daring to invent	**10** Beyond pride Clarifying your desires	**18** Beyond fate Weaving a new future	**26** Beyond delaying or avoiding Expressing honest responses
3 Beyond expectation Accepting surprises	**11** Beyond holding on Beginning again	**19** Beyond ambivalence Acting on deeper commitments	**27** Beyond persuasion Offering and inviting
4 Beyond self-discipline Savoring spontaneous moments	**12** Beyond irritation Appreciating separate realities	**20** Beyond hope and fear Taking action, however small	**28** Beyond "hearing" Listening with alert compassion
5 Beyond fixed positions Increasing flexibility	**13** Beyond blame Embracing underlying intentions	**21** Beyond restlessness Carrying out the intention to connect	**29** Beyond swallowing back feelings Expressing yourself clearly
6 Beyond forgiveness Reinterpreting and releasing the past	**14** Beyond guilt Releasing phantoms	**22** Beyond assertiveness Acting from genuine power	**30** Beyond being articulate Speaking from innate wisdom
7 Beyond compromise Expanding the range of choices	**15** Beyond dependency Experiencing inner strength	**23** Beyond deserving Moving with trust and intention	**31** Beyond embarrassment Speaking out with honesty
8 Beyond present possibilities Exploring a larger you	**16** Beyond reacting Choosing the waves to ride	**24** Beyond struggle and effort Allowing playfulness	**32** Beyond words Communicating in silence

Your Connection with Anyone

ENJOYING FREEDOM AND ABUNDANCE	CONNECTING WITH COMPASSION	TRUSTING THE TRUE SELF	HONORING THE TRUE SELF OF OTHERS
33 Beyond fear and caution **Opening to adventure**	41 Beyond right and wrong **Recognizing the wisdom of the heart**	49 Beyond making a good impression **Radiating inner beauty**	57 Beyond superiority and inferiority **Recognizing basic nobility**
34 Beyond possessiveness **Assuring mutual freedom**	42 Beyond being reasonable **Knowing the ways of the heart**	50 Beyond confusion **Trusting your intuition**	58 Beyond agreement **Appreciating different beliefs**
35 Beyond hero worship **Appreciating your inherent qualities**	43 Beyond having things in common **Sharing the ability to envision**	51 Beyond loneliness **Discovering the self as companion**	59 Beyond tact **Acknowledging strengths**
36 Beyond seriousness **Experiencing lightness and humor**	44 Beyond pressure to do **Embracing your stillness**	52 Beyond rejection **Reconnecting with your true self**	60 Beyond attachment **Seeing the essence behind the form**
37 Beyond obligation **Living from free choice**	45 Beyond established roles **Engaging from the heart**	53 Beyond acquiescence **Respecting the authority of your true self**	61 Beyond helping **Empowering others**
38 Beyond jealousy **Releasing with a blessing**	46 Beyond relief **Experiencing delight**	54 Beyond security **Discovering inner resources**	62 Beyond anger **Honoring the deeper common purpose**
39 Beyond need **Accepting innate abundance**	47 Beyond proving **Knowing from within**	55 Beyond internal conflict **Honoring integrity**	63 Beyond competition **Cooperating out of strength**
40 Beyond control **Affirming autonomy**	48 Beyond sympathy **Acting from compassion**	56 Beyond "going somewhere" **Appreciating where you are now**	64 Beyond giving or receiving **Sharing a joyful balance**

Part I

OPENING AND EXPANDING

CHAPTER 1

Beyond Present Boundaries: Opening New Territory

Since birth each of us has opened up a great deal of territory by meeting and connecting with others. We know many people, some as family and intimates, some as friends, others as coworkers or casual acquaintances. By this time in our lives, we have each developed familiar patterns in the way we relate to others. Much of what we say and do seems so natural that we don't even notice it. But in every relationship, whether we are aware of it or not, we establish boundaries through the way we think, act, and respond.

Our boundaries keep us safe, and protect our identities as separate people, but in certain situations they hold us back. In an intimate relationship, for example, a man may establish what he hopes is a safe boundary by limiting how much of his feelings and hopes he is willing to share. But by insulating himself from possible rejection, he is also keeping the relationship from opening up and expanding. Even when we think we are being open, we can set limits in a subtle way. For example, if a woman is very generous with her time and energy, that pattern of generosity can become a boundary that closes her in and prevents her from having needed time alone.

Remember, in connecting with people, the boundaries are set not by surveyors but solely by you. Any time you feel dissatisfied with a relationship, it is a signal that you are ready to open up new territory—in the way you speak and listen and the way you perceive yourself when you are with others. It may be a signal that you are ready to understand other people in a new way. Rather than disregarding your vague disappointment, try thinking of it as a hand tapping you on the shoulder, awakening you to new possibilities.

Imagine you are entering a forest with the freedom to explore in whatever direction you desire. Before you enter, stop and consciously choose your path. Before you lie various paths—paths of joy and of compassion, of wisdom and of harmony. Be guided by your sincere desire to bridge your feelings of separation from others, or your feelings of isolation when alone. As you walk, notice the moments when your spirit lifts. Those moments are your assurance that you are on the path toward fulfillment.

All the paths in life's forest are connected. So long as you walk with deliberate and free choice, you will never get lost for long. When you get distracted, pause until you regain an inner sense of the right path to choose. Then turn in that direction and begin again. As you consciously choose each day which path you enjoy most, you will find that your interactions with other people become more satisfying and your time alone more rewarding. This ease with yourself and with others is your birthright. You have only to claim it.

1. Think of a specific relationship you have now. Imagine how it might be better if it moved beyond its present boundaries. Imagine allowing yourself to step over the boundaries of familiar words and actions and take a different path the next time you are together.

2. Spend 5 minutes thinking of ways you might think, feel, speak, and act differently in this relationship. Be prepared to discover new ways of connecting.

3. Begin a journal of your new connections by describing the path you have chosen. What does it look like? How do you feel when you walk on it? Does it have a name (e.g., "Openness," "Delight")? Write what happened when you tried out your new ideas.

Keep your journal as you progress through this book. You can refer back to your favorite results, and remind yourself how successful you have been. You'll be surprised and delighted to see how far you've come.

CHAPTER 2

Beyond Practicality: Daring to Invent

Doing things the same way every time can save time and energy. But if you think of something you'd love to do and hear yourself saying, "I would really enjoy that, but it's just not practical," stop and reflect. Perhaps there is a way of doing it you haven't thought of. All sorts of things become possible if you use your ingenuity.

Unfortunately, those who dare to invent have almost always met with resistance at first. Could you be resisting your own creative side? Nearly everything we do can be enhanced, amplified, and made more joyful by our own inventiveness. From the moment we awake each morning, we can fill our days with new and interesting people, our minds with new ideas, our work with creativity.

Our inventive spirit can reach up and bring our dearest desires into our lives. Yet we often hold this side back. We were rewarded for being practical as we grew up, and practicality still rules most of us. Once we teach our inventive and practical sides to work together, they will help us not only with everyday tasks, but to make true connections with the people with whom we wish to share our ideas, our work, and our lives.

If a relationship truly has value to you, dare to try out new ways to expand and revitalize it. Invent points of special contact each day—a touch of encouragement, a moment of eye-to-eye contact, an activity that stimulates relaxation and laughter. Inventiveness requires the ability to see a situation or person from a different angle; so do all you can to vary your point of view. Try swinging together in the park, lying upside down, walking barefoot, anything that pulls you out of the ordinary. Throwing a large ball back and forth can be fun; doing it while treading water in a pool opens you to laughter.

If you think of yourself as a person of amazing ingenuity, occasions will appear that give you the chance to prove it. You'll reach your desires through inventiveness and sustain them through practicality.

The more you stretch your imagination in small ways, the more creative you will become in major areas of your life. Think of occasions when you have used ingenuity to put together a quick, sumptuous meal out of whatever food you had in the house. Or create a "vacation" for mind and body without going away from home. Everyone has the capacity to invent new experiences, new ways of seeing and hearing other people.

Each time you're inventive you experience a new part of yourself. Each new doorway that you dare to go through leads into a room filled with surprises. Most intriguing of all, everything you invent that gives you a deeper sense of joy is also a gift to those closest to you. As you expand your inventiveness, you'll develop a more confident sense of who you are, and you'll become a more interesting friend, a more enjoyable companion. Your interest in creating new ways to be with your friends, or to accomplish your work, will stimulate you and everyone around you. Enlivening a relationship that once was monotonous is like stepping out into the sunshine after a spell of rain.

1. In 3 minutes or less, tell a friend your life story—but tell it from the viewpoint that you have always been amazingly creative and full of ingenuity in every area of your life. Choose events that support this idea, and recount them with delight in the fact that you are a very inventive person. While you speak, your partner should remain silent. Then let him tell his story in the same way. After this game, you will find new memories bubbling up for the next few days, validating the fact that you *have* always been an unusually inventive person.

2. Choose an area of a relationship (e.g., sharing meals together) that could use revitalizing, and think up unusual, even outrageous new ways to enliven it. Select the best of your ideas, refine them, and put your whole self into carrying them out.

3. When you have achieved success in one area, use your ingenuity in another. Your personal or professional situation, your leisure time —every area of your life can be transformed when you apply inventiveness to it.

CHAPTER 3

Beyond Expectation: Accepting Surprises

When we decide we want something, and decide we want someone else to give it to us, we create an expectation. We begin with what seems like a pleasant idea. As we play with the idea, we pour more of our energy into it until it becomes a conviction. Soon we feel we are *entitled* to what we want—happiness, approval, security—and that a particular person should provide it. Once we begin to feed this conviction, we develop very strong feelings. In the end we feel slighted, even insulted, if the other person doesn't meet our expectations.

In connecting with other people, look for your unconscious expectations. Often they are hidden just below the surface. One way to discover these is to say to yourself, "If I did have an expectation I am not aware of, it would be ———." Surprisingly, the answer will often pop right into your mind.

Once you are able to put your expectations into words, they can be clearly spelled out for both of you to see. Unacknowledged expectations confuse and separate. They also create a powerful resistance in the people we are trying to relate to. For example, if I expected a friend to spend a certain amount of time with me each week, and that didn't happen, I would feel disappointed. Even if I tried to hide my disappointment, my friend would sense it. Either he would spend less time than ever with me, or, if he did meet my expectation in order to keep peace between us, I would be even more disappointed that I got the expected time and yet did not experience the delight I had anticipated.

No matter how ridiculous expectations may sound when expressed, or how foolish we may feel in acknowledging them, it takes only a moment of discomfort to do so. I often start by saying, "I know this may sound ridiculous to you, but I've discovered that I expect that ——— will happen when we are together. You don't have to respond to my expectation; but I feel better expressing it." This clears the air. I also may acknowledge that my expectations are probably influenced by a movie, my early childhood, a dream. Who knows where our expectations come from?

In an intimate relationship, be as specific as possible about what you have been expecting. If you want to feel loved, state exactly how you would "know" if you were. In a relationship with a coworker, share your vision of working together with harmony and enjoyment.

When you become aware of someone else's expectations of you, ask yourself whether you share that person's vision and would enjoy fulfilling that expectation together. Half-hearted efforts to meet each other's expectations are worse than no efforts. They use up our energy and create disappointment. It takes much more energy to do something when we do it merely to meet someone's expectation of us. We end up "foot-dragging"—we drag our feet in getting dressed, or completing a project, or coming back from lunch when we do it to meet someone else's expectation. If foot-dragging becomes a habit, we may start believing it is a normal way to live.

Our expectations of ourselves get us into just as much trouble. They are like blinders that limit us to tunnel vision. We can't be spontaneous and creative, because we can't see anything but the outcome we expect. Who can think creatively when disappointment could be just around the corner? We are at our most creative when we are open to whatever comes.

To move from expectation to surprise, notice the repeating pattern that you have set up—you have a nice idea, you turn that idea into an expectation, the response is not what you expected, you end up feeling disappointed. Once you become aware of the pattern you can begin to drop your expectations, one at a time. As you do, you will begin to take pleasure in each moment. That's when surprises happen.

1. List several expectations you have of a person, your family, a boss, or a coworker—that he or she should be more appreciative, more loving, pay you more money, be more cheerful, prompt, understanding.

2. Examine each expectation. Try seeing it as something that you made up and have believed "should be" delivered to you. Cross out each expectation that you can see from this new viewpoint and are willing to let go of now.

3. Imagine that surprises, far beyond your expectations, are circling overhead—like airplanes waiting for clearance to land. Each expectation that you can release makes room on the field for another surprise.

CHAPTER 4

Beyond Self-Discipline: Savoring Spontaneous Moments

At times we all criticize ourselves for lack of self-discipline, and resolve to push ourselves harder. Often, however, it is not ourselves, but our situation that needs changing. The less a project or relationship causes your spirits to rise, the more self-discipline it requires. A project that is not animated by the rhythm of your delight has to be pushed by great effort.

When we lack a sense of purpose in our work or relationships we continually have to force ourselves on with self-reproach to avoid feeling lazy, irresponsible, immature. Ask yourself what would happen if you simply stopped forcing yourself into lifeless situations and relationships. If you are involved in a project that you are forcing yourself to complete, but you know it will be satisfying in the long run, then the extra little shove self-discipline gives will be welcome. In any long-term project or relationship, about 20 percent self-discipline added to 80 percent enthusiasm can sustain your natural rhythm when your energy flags.

Some people use self-discipline to get up in the morning, to organize their day, turn off the television, or eat nutritious food. Acquiring a new habit may call for 40 to 50 percent self-discipline—to get going on an aerobics program, to lose weight, to reach past an old boundary of isolation.

But excessive self-pushing can quickly become self-punishing. If you find yourself caught in a grind of endless pressure to keep going, you can call a halt. Many people foolishly wait until they can use their doctor's authority ("He has to rest"; "She is a very sick woman"); others make a half-hearted effort to continue, feeling they must be "responsible." But their attitude of weariness is apparent and affects everyone else's enthusiasm. Rather than wait until your body is too exhausted to continue, or your emotions have dulled your life spirit, you can responsibly stop what you are doing. Before you lose your connection (personal or professional) with others out of sheer exhaustion, speak up honestly and take responsibility for the consequences of your action. For example, if you find yourself in over your head on a project, you can say, "I thought I could work well on this project when I began it, but for several weeks I have not felt any genuine interest or enthusiasm in it. I would like to make a fair arrangement with you to withdraw my participation." You will be relieved, and your reputation will not be marred by work that is not up to standard.

When you free yourself from the drudgery of joyless activities you open the door to spontaneous ideas that come to you as you go about your day. Your work will take on a sense of delight and true purpose. Whether you are shoveling snow out of the driveway, teaching your child to spell, or planning a new sanctuary for migrant birds, you will feel energized.

Be receptive to your lighthearted impulses. Welcome spontaneous ideas. They often offer opportunities to relate to people in ways that fan the flame of your own natural energy.

To someone else you may appear to be working longer and harder than ever before, but to you it will feel different. As you work on projects you are genuinely interested in and spend your time with others in ways that you all want, you will find that work is joyful and time flies by quickly.

1. Examine one area in your life in which you are using a hefty amount of self-discipline to keep going. (It could be your running program, your eating regime, your sleeping time, your evenings, your budget, your household maintenance, your entire career.) Ask yourself what belief bars the door to spontaneous enjoyment?

2. If you were to act with joyful spontaneity in that situation, what would happen? And if that happened, what would happen next? And if *that* came to pass, what would result?

3. Think of one situation in which you have acted through spontaneous inspiration without the least need for self-discipline, in which the result was not only joyful but also far-reaching and satisfying for everyone involved. Remember your sense of deeper purpose as you acted, and how much fun you had.

CHAPTER 5

Beyond Holding a Fixed Position: Increasing Flexibility

We think that our convictions grow out of our experiences in life, but many of our experiences actually shape themselves to fit our fixed positions. For example, if I should decide that an employee is irresponsible —and lose the flexibility to see that person as responsible—then no matter how hard he tried to prove his worth, I would continue to find him irresponsible. Or, as one client told me, "Once I took the position that Robert loved me deeply and had only my best interests at heart, I experienced all his actions as proof of my position. If he called me at 1:00 A.M. from a distant time zone, it proved that he loved me so much he couldn't wait until the next morning. If he didn't call for a couple of days, I knew he loved me so much that he couldn't bear to interrupt my sleep."

Most of our viewpoints are continually expanding and incorporating new ideas. But sometimes we unwittingly cut ourselves off from our experiences and our viewpoints lose their flexibility. They control our life experiences and form a wall that separates us from others. When this happens we miss out on potential friendships with delightful, intelligent, and caring people who have positions that don't match ours, or who fall into a group (bright women, sweet women, sensitive men, macho men) to which we have closed our minds.

If you hold on to any position without adding to, deleting, or modifying it in some way through the years, that belief is probably going to direct (and perhaps limit) your experience with the people you meet. "Never trust a stranger," "Women are more emotional than men," or "Children don't understand" will subtly separate you from realizing the potential of each person you meet.

We can trap ourselves in our set positions. The more we defend them, the more likely we are to hang on to them past their usefulness to us. We hesitate to change because we feel foolish throwing away a belief we have staunchly defended. It's hard to admit—or even believe—that positions we cling to with conviction today may change completely six months from now.

Look at some strong positions you have held for a long time. You will probably find that they fall into two broad categories: those we experience as the truth for us—even though they may not be true for someone else—and those we have adopted from outside our own experience. The ones we *know,* from our own experience, we don't even bother to defend (e.g., "My relationship with my wife works better when she feels independent, strong, and powerful." "I feel better when I exercise outdoors." "I feel peaceful and calm in the mountains"). Ironically, the positions that are less central are the ones we get stubborn about (e.g., "All women should enjoy being mothers." "Men have always been controlled by women").

We generally cling to a particular belief, not when our footing is secure, but when we are working to keep or regain our balance. Perhaps we have always followed the authority of others, and are just beginning to learn to discriminate and choose for ourselves. As we make the transition, we are naturally wary of too much flexibility. It's a challenge just to recognize the difference between deferring to someone else's position and listening carefully in order to learn from his or her viewpoints.

You can learn to evaluate your own cherished positions and to appreciate opposing views by playing a simple game. Choose an issue in which you and a friend have opposite and inflexible positions. Agree to take the other person's position for ten minutes and see what happens. Perhaps you hold opposing and equally fixed ideas about politics. Sit down together and try arguing each other's sides. If you have been stubbornly defending the Democrats, try defending the Republicans with the same enthusiasm. At first it will feel very strange to hear yourself making such "untrue" statements, but know that your friend is suffering the same identity crisis. Soon you may notice that you can act this position out with a lot of feeling and have fun doing it. You even think of points your friend has overlooked. Listening to your friend become involved in your position makes it worth the effort to think in what seems like a backward way.

This game loosens stuck positions and restores natural flexibility. The more we gain flexibility, the more we enjoy learning about other people's beliefs without feeling threatened by them. It's easy when we trust our power to choose for ourselves.

Whenever you find yourself rigidly defending an idea or an action, think of a tall pine tree in the wind, all of its branches swaying. The trunk leans a little, yet the roots remain firmly fixed, giving it stability even in high winds.

You can learn to sway in powerful winds of change with no fear of losing your balance or of disturbing your deep roots. You'll discover the wide range of views people have of the world, many sprung from the roots of intuitive knowledge. As you regain your natural flexibility and find fresh stimulation and enthusiasm in your relationships, you will suddenly see ideas and possibilities that were invisible before.

1. Think of a recent time when you took a strong stand on an issue. What was the result of this stance? Was this particular position useful to you at one point in your life?
2. Now consider the original reason you took this fixed position. How might you make the same point, yet be open and flexible enough to allow new refinements? How have your personal experiences already expanded your views from your original stand on that issue?
3. Replay the situation you chose in step 1 in your mind. This time, imagine yourself with a more open approach that allows you to expand or alter your position the next time it comes up.

CHAPTER 6

Beyond Forgiveness: Reinterpreting and Releasing the Past

Imagine a child who spends long hours laboriously building a house of cards with his friends. The house proves unstable and trembles at approaching footsteps, and it eventually collapses. No one needs to be forgiven for the house's downfall. Wiser from their experience the children enthusiastically start building a stronger foundation for their next house.

Whatever we resent and cannot forgive interrupts the flow of our lives. If we feel like victims we spend our precious time and energy mentally going over and over what happened.

Our most intense and frequent thoughts often are reflected back to us by other people. If we are unwilling to forgive, we find ourselves surrounded by unforgiving people. We can free ourselves to belong to a mutually forgiving group of friends only by learning to reinterpret—and thereby forgive—our past.

Think of an event in your life, whether yesterday or years ago, when you felt that someone took advantage of you. Ask yourself what was your first inkling that things might not turn out as you wanted? Was there something that you thought of doing about it but decided not to do? Be precise about the moment you decided *not* to take action—when you chose to take a chance that things would work out. Did you think, "I had better check this man's story?" Or, "maybe I should get this in writing." Or, "I have a hunch this woman is leading me on . . ."? The moment you delayed appropriate action was the moment you might have changed the undesirable outcome, but didn't. Until you find those moments when your action *might* have made a difference, it's hard to forgive or forget. Whenever we don't acknowledge our part in the outcome of a situation, we can't let go of it.

If you realize that you participated (in no matter how small a way) in setting up the unwanted outcome, you can reinterpret and release the event. Only by seeing the situation differently can you digest the kernel of wisdom gained and toss away the shell in which it was delivered. Think how funny you would look walking down the street with your pockets bulging with empty pecan shells. Each situation that requires forgiveness is like a pecan shell. Once you crack it open and take out the nut of wisdom inside, you can throw away the shell.

If you feel anger toward yourself you'll forgive yourself as soon as you realize you are wiser now and won't make that mistake again. Once you are convinced the situation won't be repeated—whoosh—you can forgive yourself—just like that. One act of forgiveness to yourself can set off a chain reaction; soon you will find yourself forgiving others as well. If one experience of forgiveness can give you a new start in a relationship, ten can catapult you into true delight.

When you forgive others you give a gift to yourself. Suddenly there are no villains and no victims—only people who are free to choose wisely and well.

1. For practice, try one small act of forgiveness. Write down the end result of a situation that made you angry (e.g., "He didn't bring my car back"; "She left without saying a word").

2. When did you have your first inkling that the situation might not work out as you wanted? What action did you consider taking before you decided to take a chance that things would come out all right? Did you think, "What if he doesn't return my car? Maybe I should ask him to rent one"? Or, "I wonder if I should talk to her and find out what is wrong?"

3. Write down what you decided instead of taking the action you considered. "No, I hate to seem selfish—surely he will return my car tomorrow." Or, "What if she makes demands? I'll just wait it out and hope for the best." If you have any difficulty seeing how you helped to set yourself up as a victim, ask a friend to listen and help you look for clues while you reenact the situation.

4. Describe what you feel about the situation now, as you see the action you might have taken and didn't. You may not be sure whether your input could have changed the outcome, but even the slightest doubt, once acknowledged, will shift you away from feeling like a totally helpless victim.

CHAPTER 7

Beyond Compromise: Expanding the Range of Choices

Imagine the discomfort of two furniture movers, who disagree on the best way to lift a piano into their van, straining to hold the piano as they work out a compromise. Compromise is an art, and it can offer a way out of conflict—especially when you and another person are locked in struggle over two ways to proceed. But working out a compromise can also delay or obstruct your purpose together—it can cause you to feel noble or sacrificial, or leave you with the suspicion that a better agreement might have been possible.

Instead of limiting yourself to either-or situations, you can expand your range of choices. For example, if you are in a business or personal conflict, go beyond the immediate problem and ask yourself what is your highest purpose in working or being with the other person. As soon as you identify the real purpose, new choices will unfold before you. Don't say no to any of them, no matter how unexpected they seem. Examine each one in a spirit of adventure. Look for the action that will allow you to settle the conflict and move on.

If the decision seems important (how much difference will it make in a year or five years?), take time alone to think through all the possibilities. You will intuitively know which alternative is best—it will be the one that makes you feel the most confident when you think about it. If you are tempted to settle for a secure or dutiful choice, imagine carrying out that choice. How would you feel about the results? The decision that gives you the most energy and joy will best serve you and everyone else involved.

One part of you may think that free choice is irresponsible, an escape from your obligations. All the sides of yourself want to help you live your life more fully, so talk to your hesitant part and show it your purpose in the present conflict. After you have explored all your options, meet with the other person and discuss the discoveries you are most excited about. Every time you encourage new insights, more choices will pop up. They arise from all of your past experiences and surface spontaneously when you let go of the old choices that once served you.

A delightful way for two people to come together on a point of disagreement is to list all the choices you could both be happy with. For example, two partners disagreed over how to divide ownership of their business. One wanted 80 percent of the business, but the other felt that 50 percent each was more fair. As a first step toward agreement they added 10 percent to the 50 and took 10 percent from the 80. Then just 10 percent divided them. They wrote 60 percent, 65 percent, and 70 percent on three slips of paper. One partner put each slip under a shell, and the other partner prepared to draw. They agreed that both would abide by—and would even feel blessed by—the percentage drawn. After the drawing they signed an agreement and went out to celebrate their new beginning.

By increasing their choices, they eliminated the need for either to lose face, to be made wrong by the other, or to be manipulated through subtle threat or charm. The conflict was over before it could escalate. They were free to bring new ideas into their partnership.

1. Think of a situation in your life that could be improved through expanding your range of choices.
2. Lie down and imagine that you are gently swinging in a hammock strung between two trees by the side of a lake. As you lie there gently swinging in the breeze, feel the sun warm your face. Allow yourself to go into a deeper and deeper state of relaxation. As your mind becomes still, you will be even more receptive to new choices. It is as if you were inviting ideas to come floating into your mind, just as the leaves occasionally fall from the trees above you.
3. Let the sun be a symbol for the best possible choices for everyone involved in the situation. Do not be concerned if you seem to fall asleep for a moment. The new choices will be there when you awaken.

CHAPTER 8

Beyond Present Possibilities: Exploring a Larger You

Remember the excitement you felt each time you traveled farther away than you had ever been before—whether to the next town or another continent? You've experienced that excitement over and over again. Most of us travel freely in the world without asking permission, yet we hesitate to explore the larger world of our own being without permission —and encouragement—from others. We *do* need permission for this kind of exploration, but no one can give it to us except ourselves.

The roles you play now—or, as some prefer to say, the roles life "has cast you in"—have become familiar, whether you enjoy them or not. Each role carries a set of images, or beliefs, about yourself. You are a "mother," a "husband," a "good provider," a "creative person," and so on. These beliefs form the boundaries that you have set, and within which you live your life. The role of wife, of husband, of lover varies tremendously from person to person, according to the boundaries each has set.

The boundaries of your roles—the lines you speak, the script you follow—have been set by you. Only you can make the choice to change them. You can expand minor roles into major ones, or drop some roles altogether. Decide which roles you really want, change the boundaries of those you don't want, and try them out again.

You will change your boundaries many times, in response to the various stages or events in your life. As a father or mother, you will move from guiding your child closely and frequently to simply modeling the kind of behavior you wish your child to have. So not only do our roles change, our behavior within the roles also changes.

If you have changed a role but still don't like it, look for a way to continue being responsible and yet act from a spontaneous sense of yourself rather than from the role. As a wife or husband you can simply relate moment-to-moment rather than according to how you think a marriage partner "should" act. You can explore your honest responses to each other in relation to your sense of purpose. Gradually, you will drop more and more roles and act entirely out of your own integrity.

When you go beyond self-imposed boundaries you will have greater freedom and renewed energy in all areas of your life. Every time you expand or drop one boundary line in your life, you affect the others as well—for your physical, emotional, and mental boundaries are all woven together, like the interwoven threads in the pattern of a fabric.

Suppose you are worried about having enough money to buy something you want. Instead of giving in to anxiety, you can explore a new boundary simply by letting go of your fears. Trust that your needs will be met as they arise. That new attitude will affect how you play your role in your business life (e.g., you'll put less pressure on yourself to make more money, to be promoted); in your relationships with your family (you'll have a generous heart, more fun in cooperating); and in your relationship with yourself (you'll be able to have enough time to be quiet and alone without the push to count your money, to project your budget).

When you focus on the larger vision and get a sense of how your life could be different, you will get a sense of the grace and warmth that can be yours. The gates to love, joy, patience, compassion—all can be opened with your desire and imagination. Rather than push against the walls of your old boundaries, find the gate and walk through it. Once you do you will experience life as if you were in a new place with new people. This is true even when you remain in the same job, or in the same living situation. Your real boundaries are your beliefs about who you are; they are not situations imposed by someone else.

No matter how loving, powerful, or wise you feel now, tomorrow even this view of yourself will be too small and restricted. As you toss out beliefs and roles you have outgrown, you will be surprised by the larger sense of *you* that remains.

Allow your passion to rise up again for the pursuit of your life dream, the one you have glimpsed on and off but set aside for some other day. When you go in the direction of the picture that inspires you, you will naturally discover a larger world of being. Outer adventures will follow the lead of your inner discoveries.

1. Explore the boundaries that restrict your mental expansion, your emotional well being, or your physical vitality. Picture yourself opening the gate and walking further into the world of your wisdom. Trust that each gateway will open as you focus on what is beyond.
2. List practical ways to connect with your vision of a quality you would like to experience. Include small steps you can take. For example, if you would like to be more patient, set a timer to go off every hour or every half hour. When it rings, check to see if you are feeling impatient. Consciously adopt an aspect of patience—such as perseverance, fortitude, pleasant rhythm of working, diligence, tolerance, steady ease, understanding, responsiveness, generosity.

3. Spend a few moments thinking about each characteristic of patience (or whatever gate you have chosen)—what it means, what it is related to, how you would know if you had it. Think about patience as often as you can for 1 week. You will be able to look back at the end of the week and see the change that you have made. If you do this for 2 weeks, you will discover an even larger picture of who you are.

Part II

CENTERING AND INTEGRATING

CHAPTER 9

Beyond Withdrawing: Finding Your True Center

All of us withdraw from time to time, shutting down our sensitivity to everyday beauty and to the people around us. Most often we simply have distractions pulling our minds away from our companions. But sometimes withdrawal comes from a deeper need. It is like a call from deep within ourselves that insists we stop to reflect on our direction in life. This kind of withdrawal affects every area of our lives; it reflects a soul hunger that friends cannot satisfy no matter how much they want to help. Only quiet time alone fills this need for withdrawal.

Both kinds of withdrawal feel trance-like. (Certainly we look like we're in a trance when we withdraw.) It's hard to know which kind we are experiencing, since the symptoms are the same—we lose interest in the person we are with, our thoughts wander to other things, we lose buoyant emotions. Withdrawal often dulls our natural pleasure in movement, too, and can send our thoughts whirling in repetitious circles. We can't enjoy other people when we feel withdrawn; we can't even enjoy ourselves.

If you feel as though you are withdrawing from someone, stop and think about what is really going on. You may simply be distracted by a concern about something else—an unfinished commitment or communication that is unrelated to the person you are with. If you briefly acknowledge the temporary distraction, or put aside a few minutes to take care of it with a phone call or a scribbled reminder, you can free yourself to *be with* the other person. Since people always know when they are not being fully heard, your companion will be as relieved as you are to get back to really being together.

If you are with another person out of a sense of obligation, social or business, your responses will be colored by your true desire to be somewhere else. And, whether he acknowledges it or not, your companion will know it, just as you know when someone is being with you only out of obligation.

In such obligatory situations both people tend to withdraw inside while appearing amiable on the outside. Ironically, many of us try to cope with the discomfort of withdrawal by talking more, feeling pressured *to do something* about it and not knowing what to do.

If you have a strong wish to be somewhere else, you can honestly say so—but first acknowledge that the cause lies in you, not the other person. Saying that your mind is on your child, family, work, car, or home— without apology, blame, or guilt—is a simple yet powerful way to lessen your need to withdraw.

If you discover that you do indeed wish to be where you are, acknowledge that you feel somewhat withdrawn, assure your friend it has nothing to do with him or her. Honestly say, "I am having doubts about spending too much money, taking too much time, being heard," or whatever the case is. You may not know for sure, but if you act on your best guess you will restore your sense of real communication.

If you have pinpointed the possible distractions, taken action on them, and still find that you are withdrawn, set aside some time each day to spend alone in a tranquil state. Try to get a perspective on exactly what is happening—or changing or developing—in your life. Then choose the path that will help you move in the direction you want to go.

1. Recall the last time you felt withdrawn when you were with some-one. Imagine how you might have acknowledged your distraction without guilt, apology, or blame.
2. See yourself speaking honestly to the other person about what you would rather have been doing at the moment. Practice until you feel you have found the best way to express it.
3. Set aside time to do what you really want to do—but have avoided doing—in the coming week. If you have been wanting to be alone and to reflect on the direction of your life, set a time to do so and hold it inviolate.

CHAPTER 10

Beyond Pride: Clarifying Your Desires

Pride is one of the easiest emotions to understand. It comes out of fear, sometimes only a small fear. It usually springs from the thought that you are "not as good as" someone else. Pride can make its appearance in your life in a series of fascinating costumes. It may dress in the best wine labels, the sportiest car, the status of a title, the shimmer of a trophy. Ironically, anything you buy or attain to *prove* that you are now "okay" will separate you from those who don't have the same thing, yet it will not truly connect you with those who do.

The longer you have believed you need a particular thing in order to be "good enough," the more pride you will feel when you have it—and the more it will distance you from others. In contrast, when you acquire something out of simple delight and enjoyment, it does not diminish closeness with others.

In relationships, pride always separates. Clarity about what you desire or who you are helps you to connect. Learn to recognize the difference between pride and clarity. Pride attempts to hold together an already shaky self-esteem; clarity enhances your sense of your true self. When you are clear about your own goals and desires, you will also want others to attain theirs. This attitude will lead you naturally into closer friendships.

Overcoming pride means not only sharing with others, but also being willing to receive from them. If you are eager to give to others without really being open to receive, you are saying in effect that you have more to give than they do, even though that is not what you mean to communicate. If you want to learn to receive without letting pride get in your way, try giving as little as you possibly can this week and decide to be open to accept whatever gifts come your way.

When you realize that some kind of fear lurks behind each area of pride, you can begin to dissolve your pride by observing your fears. You may fear being criticized—by others or by yourself—or you may fear "failing" in some way. Whenever you discover that a part of you feels fearful or cornered, be gentle with it. You can speak with that part of yourself, even carry on a conversation with it. Write down what this facet of your personality wants from you as well as what you want from it. Offer it encouragement. Agree to its reasonable requests.

Fear can be soothed and gentled in any area of your life, and when it is, your pride begins to dissolve. You will feel as if a weight has fallen off your shoulders. As you become more comfortable with all parts of yourself, your ease of spontaneous expression will surprise even you.

1. Choose one area of your life in which you take special pride—even a little—because of your knowledge, understanding, accomplishments, or possessions, or your spiritual, mental, or physical development. If you can't think of an area, finish the sentence, "Well, at least, I am *not* proud about ———," and look at that one.

2. Imagine that everyone you know has the same quality or honor you are proud of. See if this shifts your feeling. If your delight increases, notice the new connection you are feeling with the people who have what you have.

3. Think about what you dream of doing with your life, beyond the expectations of others. Allow ideas to flow, ideas that may have been pushed back so that families or friends would be "proud" of you. Keep these ideas in your mind for as long as you can each day, whether it's 2 minutes or 2 hours.

CHAPTER 11

Beyond Holding On: Beginning Again

If you are holding on to a person or to a situation—say a spouse or a job —simply because it seems frightening to let go, you are not alone. We have all been there before and know the feeling. Each time we have let go of something familiar, we've wondered whether we would ever find anything so good again. But when we gather inner strength to see the next possibility, somehow it always brings more fulfillment than we have known before.

In relationships, we sometimes avoid letting go by saying that the other person would be lost without us. Perhaps the other person is silently thinking that we would be hurt, even devastated, if the relationship were to break up. Each of us has hit upon the ultimate insult—the belief that another person is too weak and helpless to create a new and happy life on his or her own.

We have all felt the loss of energy and enthusiasm in a group that continues to meet even though there is nothing more to be accomplished together. Only when one member courageously speaks up to acknowledge the situation do the others sigh with relief and then begin to say "thank you" and mean it.

As you become more and more sensitive to your true response to others, you will know when it's time to let go of anything in a relationship that is no longer working. Look for these signs: dreading or not enjoying the time spent together; frequently complaining about the other person, silently or to your friends; feeling resentments stack up; seeing faults more readily than virtues in the other person. You may discover that the longer you are together on a day-to-day basis, the less of your life energy you want to share.

It often helps to spend time apart from each other. It may take a few days or even several months to let go of old images and negative feelings. Be willing to let go of the past and become reacquainted with your real self. You may choose to end your present form of connecting—marriage, partnership, close friendship. If so, why not do so with a sense of joyful anticipation that leaves the door open to begin a new relationship together?

Once you each release outworn images of yourselves, you will be free to see a different person in front of you. Old expectations disappear and a feeling of discovery returns. You'll each see the other's face look more alive. Free people who choose to be together look different from people who hold on to ways of relating that don't bring delight. Even your partner's body will somehow look taller, more graceful and attractive. You are likely to notice that you have new respect for his or her time, ideas, and self-expression. And you will be free to respond fully. Possibly, new names for each other will help to mark the transition, since the old names hold old images that no longer fit.

Your new connection will be based on new images of who both of you are. You will discover delight and appreciation you could not possibly have experienced while restricted by the old images. The length of time you stay apart is not crucial. What matters is that both of you eagerly look ahead rather than behind.

As you become clearer about your purpose in being together and about what gifts you have for each other, you can connect in ways that bring you closer.

For example, only do together what is joyful or offers the fulfillment of a deeper purpose. If he likes football and you detest the game, or you love opera and she sleeps through it, share these interests with other friends instead.

Be courageous. Let go of all established patterns of being together that no longer give energy to the relationship. Even if you are holding on in a single area, such as cooking dinner when you don't want to, let go. There are countless other ways to eat well and truly enjoy the process.

Express your real desires and responses to each other. Ironically, as soon as you speak freely about your responses, positive feelings that had been hidden come bubbling up.

Decide you are going to be your total self. At the same time, encourage your partner to grow and expand toward her or his highest possible path. You will find a new kind of connection, not only with each other but with your self as well.

1. Think of a relationship in which you are holding on to a pattern that doesn't delight you. Be specific about what you are holding on to and how it has served you. Feel a wave of appreciation for your perseverance and your insight. Then imagine shedding the old pattern as a snake sheds its skin.
2. Picture the new beginning you want, and see yourself opening to receive it. Vividly imagine this picture. Step into the shoes of your future self and get a sense of what it feels like.

CHAPTER 12

Beyond Irritation: Appreciating Separate Realities

Imagine yourself standing on a ridge. You can see that it is raining in the valley to your left. People are darting for shelter. In the valley to your right the sun is shining brightly. People there are planting in their gardens. These realities differ, but from your position you can observe both of them. When you are irritated with someone whose viewpoint differs from yours, consider that you may be dwelling in different valleys.

People often assume they share the same viewpoints simply because they share the same physical space. Imagine sitting down at a café with an acquaintance. He sees clouds gathering and says the day will be dreary; you see the same clouds as a sign of a cool, pleasant day. Any further conversation between you will probably create mutual irritation because of your separate views of reality.

We often try to avoid irritation by staying in our own valleys. When we feel depressed, we seek someone who feels the same. When we feel productive and creative, we look for someone who shares that reality. These are temporary, even momentary differences. Basic differences in reality, however, can make it very difficult for two people to live in harmony.

Suppose you trust people, but your friend does not. It would be important for you to determine whether her lack of trust is due to a temporary misunderstanding or if it comes from a lack of trust in the world. If it is a surface irritation, it can lift dramatically when you help your friend to see the larger context. If your reality systems differ on a basic level, however, you will probably have a difficult time learning to communicate clearly.

You may also have conflict within yourself—the various parts of yourself may all be living in different valleys. Ask your true self to stand on a ridge and assess the situation. Then find ways to open communication between the various valleys within the landscape of yourself. As you link them together in the service of your single most important vision, conflict and irritation will diminish.

As you realize that there is always more than one reality, and that you can enter and leave them at will, the richer and more creative your life will be. As you integrate all the sides of your personality and thus begin to direct your life from your true center, you will find it easier to explore and to connect with a variety of people. Rather than rejecting their reality systems in case they might somehow invalidate your own, you will find that you go toward people, seeking to know more about how they see themselves and the world around them.

In this spirit, step into other reality systems with the assistance of those who live in them. Learn all that you can. Look for the clues that point to the deeper essence beneath the outer words. Observe the common bond between you.

As you develop this interest in other realities, you will expand and enlarge your own. You will lose nothing of value, and what you add will make your own reality richer and more complete.

1. Think of a small irritation within yourself that has distracted you. What part of your personality does this annoyance come from? Can you see the two different reality systems at work within yourself?

2. Look for ways to integrate this part into your larger self. Imagine a conversation with it, in which you explain the higher vision; or take it along as your companion on a walk in a meadow. Get an image of this part of yourself that has a different reality, and imagine it wants to help you but does not yet know how.

3. Imagine the harmony within as you come to know and to appreciate the separate realities within your own self. Gradually, you will find ways to harmonize each of these realities with your sense of true purpose.

CHAPTER 13

Beyond Blame: Embracing Underlying Intentions

When the sun glints on water, the surface can fascinate your eye even as it blocks a deeper view. Likewise, blame dazzles us with what seems immediate and real, while blinding us to what lies underneath.

We tend to blame other people for almost anything, but especially for our unhappiness. Although we try to remember which blame goes where, we soon get caught up in the melee of our blaming and turn it upon ourselves. We bounce it back and forth from self to other like a tennis ball slammed across the net. Once in play, the blame ball hits both sides of the court with equal force. It's no wonder we feel separated from our friends. While the ball is in the air, we can't stop to remember who served it. Love does not easily pour forth from slamming, whether balls or blame.

Where does blame come from? From the assumption that when something goes wrong, someone must be at fault. Finger-pointing is the next step. If the fault isn't ours, it must be the other person's, and if it isn't his or hers, it must be ours. As crazy as this reasoning is, blaming *seems* easier than simply letting go of the idea of "fault."

If the legal profession recognizes no-fault divorces and no-fault accidents, surely we can have no-fault disagreements. In every situation we do and say what seems to be the best thing at the time, given our fears, hopes, goals, background, and experience. So do our friends, enemies, and lovers. If someone sees two choices of how to act or speak—one full of warmth and compassion and the other thoughtless and insensitive—he or she would not knowingly choose the second best. Each of us does the best we can, given the options we actually experience at the moment.

No-fault thinking changes our view dramatically. If we look deep enough, we find that the people we blame for their blunders and blustering only want us to recognize them, to care about them, and to let them give their care to us. Sometimes we have to look very deep, but the intention is there waiting for us to discover it.

Your daughter defies your authority, your son is out all night, your husband falls asleep minutes after dinner, your wife is at a retreat. "This is the real world," you say. "What do you mean, no-fault?" Look again. Behind every outrageous, even seemingly thoughtless action, is a coded request for our two basic needs—love and freedom.

Talk about your underlying intentions together. Say each one as it pops up. Soon another one will pop up, and another. Each intention is real, yet it rests on top of a deeper one. When you reach the deepest one, you'll understand each other and yourself better. You won't even miss the excitement of blame as you let in more of who you are.

1. Think about the last person you blamed for something. What do you think his or her actual intention was? If it was to harm you, why would you want to continue a relationship with that person? If you think he or she made an honest mistake, then get together and talk about your deeper intentions in the relationship.

2. Trade roles with the person you blamed and replay the situation as if you had been very wise and loving beings at the time. Start where the discord began and take it to the present.

3. Describe to each other how you will handle similar situations in the future, using all the skills of your wiser characters.

CHAPTER 14

Beyond Guilt: Releasing Phantoms

Guilt is useful—for about ten minutes. We need it just long enough to call our attention to the fact that there's a better way to respond the next time. A one-year-old baby falls down after two steps, sits still for a minute, pulls herself upright, and takes two more steps. She hasn't learned to think of herself as a failure, to feel guilty, and lose her exultant spirit. As a result, the child will soon learn to walk with confidence.

Guilt comes when we fall short of what we know is possible when we give and receive love. It dissolves only when we reach out to connect using our highest visions. We all have an intuitive feeling of what a balanced relationship means. If you envision a relationship of more humor with your father, of greater mutual respect with your business partner, of open appreciation of your friend, and of deep gratitude with your marriage partner, go toward them with those pictures in mind.

Watch out for pseudo-guilt, brought on by feelings that you haven't handled your life according to someone else's direction. To extinguish pseudo-guilt, you must establish your boundaries with each person. These boundaries can always be expanded and changed, but both people need to understand what the other needs. Be specific. If your friend wants to spend seven evenings a week with you, and you're not sure whether you'd prefer three or five evenings, you will feel either guilty or resentful —neither you nor your friend can win.

Guilt that lasts longer than a few minutes is a phantom—the delusion that "more guilt is better." If this happens, the facet of your personality that likes to judge is taking over and punishing you with repeated recriminations.

Such action is woefully unjust. If it happens to you, this part of you probably hasn't learned how to balance judgments. If it metes out only sentences that obstruct your joy, retrain this part of yourself to offer you congratulations and compliments as well, and an occasional impassioned benediction when you respond to others according to your highest vision.

After all, the judge is working for you. You are the director of the drama of your life. Just show this part of yourself a new script and teach it some sample lines. It can ad lib from there.

You can free yourself from about half of each guilt just by speaking out honestly the moment you realize that your boundaries have been crossed. If you want more freedom from the phantoms of guilt, you will need to rewrite the past. In your imagination, go back to the moment you went off the track and begin again. Imagine that you were wise and compassionate at that time, and replay the scene—inserting new lines, new gestures, new voice tone, and new actions. See the new scene vividly, and pretend you are recording it on videotape. You now have a "master tape" that you can copy and replay when you need it in the future. When you know you can pull this master tape from your memory any time you need it and model your actions on its tone of wisdom, you will completely release the phantoms of guilt.

Your judging side will turn the projector off (the one that was showing reruns of old guilts chasing you). For a few days you may see faint outlines of the phantoms, but soon even the outline will disappear as you focus on the new video tape for each occasion that used to stand between you and your joy.

From now on, when you make a mistake and start to feel guilty, stop and say to yourself, "I am 97 percent on-course; that mistake is well within my 3 percent margin of error for the day."

1. Imagine that you are standing under a powerful waterfall. Let the clear water flow over your head and shoulders. Bring to mind phantoms of guilt, one at a time, and feel the power of the waterfall washing each one away.

2. Practice experiencing guilt before the deed rather than after it. You can do this by imagining the result of the action you're about to take, or the words you are about to speak. A feeling of guilt is your immediate clue to make a new choice and test the probable result again. When you feel refreshed by your choice, take that action.

CHAPTER 15

Beyond Dependency: Experiencing Inner Strength

The poppies bloomed profusely, turning the meadow red and orange. Some were big and open; others, which had grown in the shadow of the larger flowers, were small and weak. One day a group of children gathered the biggest flowers, leaving the smaller ones. Too weak to stand upright, they lay on the ground as if helpless. But they continued to bloom. As the sun shone directly on them, the stems gained strength and began to grow upright again.

When you live in the shadow of another you risk losing your basic inner strength. Many people never stop holding other people responsible for their personal satisfaction; they spend their entire lives feeling dependent. Anyone who is the object of this kind of dependency knows the great weight of such expectations, spoken or unspoken.

It is natural to be attracted to someone's strength, whether financial, physical, emotional, intellectual, or spiritual. But too often, instead of learning how to manifest our own strength, we count on the other person to have enough for both of us. Sooner or later we realize that we feel weaker instead of stronger in the area of our lives we have given over to another.

If you really want to achieve happiness without being dependent, you will find the courage to do it. You won't always feel strong in every part of your life, so begin with an area where you do feel strong.

Remember an occasion when you acted independently, out of your inner strength—as a mother, professional, organizer. Each memory will make you more aware of yourself as an autonomous being. When you have acted quickly in an emergency (an accident, illness, or death) or have taken a spontaneous stand for justice (over a mistreated dog, a wreckless driver) you have acted from strength. When you were sure of the value of an action, you had the strength to act. That inner strength and creativity can be expanded into every area of your life.

As you identify with these past acts, you will think of yourself as the kind of person who has the strength and courage to initiate action rather than depend on someone else to do it. Put your full strength behind *all* your actions. In this way you can establish a new identity of power that is derived from who you *are,* not from whom you are *with.*

Deep strength comes from the awareness of who you are. Only when you see yourself as strong can you relate in a way that strengthens others. The light is there within each of us. It's only a matter of being willing to open our inner eyes and see it.

True interdependence happens when two people experience their inner strength, not when one vainly attempts to hold both of them up. Interdependence is a dance of relating between two autonomous people. It comes from independence, and allows cooperation. Together you become an even stronger force in the world. Two strong people with a common purpose make a powerful and joyful combination.

One of the most profound joys of life is the experience of your own inner strength, of knowing you have available to you the strength to choose your path, moment by moment. Every small action you take out of your own strength is important. Small actions lead to major choices.

1. To experience your inner strength, think of a time when you were the one in charge of a situation—when the outcome rested solely upon your action. The specific situation need not have involved other people directly. Just remember the powerful feeling you had after you made a choice and stood by it. Hear again what you said, see yourself standing there, and feel your sense of balance as you handled whatever came up.

2. Imagine that you have a very wise and compassionate consultant who is an expert in the field where you feel dependent. Move to another chair and look at the chair where you were sitting. Assume the role of the wise consultant and teach the "you" that was sitting in the now empty chair. Speak simply, but in detail. Show the you in the empty chair how to bring skills from other areas of life into the area in question. Write down or tape your consultant's advice.

CHAPTER 16

Beyond Reacting: Choosing the Waves to Ride

Have you ever seen surfers sitting on their boards in the ocean, waiting for the right wave? They let several waves roll by before they suddenly swing into action, paddling to gain momentum as a wave swells, then standing up and catching the crest for a joyous ride. Their skill lies not only in moving with certainty and grace when the right wave comes, but also in knowing how to wait and let lesser or inappropriate waves go by.

In any interaction, you can choose the waves you wish to catch. You are not obligated to ride a given wave just because it's there, or to fall into somebody else's emotional cross-current.

When you react to someone else instead of responding to your own feelings and desires, you are controlled by that person's mood. Suppose a friend is grouchy and blames you for losing something. If you simply react you will defend yourself, turn the blame on him, and become just as irritable as he is. If you respond slowly and consciously, you can remember who you are and acknowledge your desire to find the lost item too—yet not get caught up in his emotional state.

When two people react to each other, rather than respond to their own centered sense of themselves, they bounce their anxiety back and forth, escalating it each time. But as soon as you realize you are reacting to the other person's anger or fear, not your own, you can move past reacting. You can let the wave of anxiety go by, resisting the impulse to be drawn into it, and wait for another wave of feeling or thought—one that promises an enjoyable ride.

When someone makes a statement, we make lightning-fast calculations in order to interpret the words and make meaning. ("She says she wants time alone—that means she's tired of me—wants to get rid of me—doesn't love me.") These interpretations are usually so rapid that they seem like the truth of what was said, rather than what they are—your personal interpretations. Teach yourself to step back to get a larger perspective. When you take a moment before you react, you will be able to respond wisely and you won't be pulled off your calm center.

If you think about it, you will see that you have done this many times. When you feel truly joyful, you don't let people who are emotionally down or upset pull you into their mood. Instead, you simply let that wave go by. Then, when it is appropriate, you initiate calm and compassionate conversation that reflects your own feelings.

Whenever you reach out from the center of who you are, you touch a similar place in the other person. People respond to you from their own deeper thoughts.

Always be ready to reach out and offer the gift of a thought. Say how beautiful the sunset is, how happy you are to see your friend, or something equally uncomplicated. Just be sure that what you say is something that has touched you. Listen to the other person's response. If it's not on the level where you wish to connect, be like the surfers and simply let it go by. A second response will follow the first. Wait for it. It may come closer to the kind of wave that you want to ride. When you wait in the knowledge that the right wave will come, filled with good feeling and surprise, you wait in a spirit of appreciation and patience.

The waves of love come in an infinite variety of forms. Each one has the power to bring out the best in both of you, and offer fulfillment beyond any you have known before. The joy of catching one is worth waiting for.

1. Think of a person to whom you have reacted in the past. Choose a person you really like, but who sometimes upsets your emotional calm by something he or she says or does.

2. Imagine that you are with this person now and he or she sends out a wave of anger. See yourself stand back, watch the wave, choose to let it go by, and remain anchored in your own reality. Listen without comment. Wait with calm for another wave—one that will offer both of you a chance to explore and delight in who you are.

Part III

ACTING FROM INTENTION

CHAPTER 17

Beyond Spending Time Together: Choosing to Connect

How long can you wait to make a real and joyful connection with someone you care about, or with a new acquaintance? In one sense, as long as you live. But the opportunity is enhanced when you are really *connecting* with people instead of just "passing time" together. With the people who matter most to you, try acting as if each time together is your last.

Like a mountain river our days flow by rapidly, but there are brief moments in every day that offer the opportunity to reach out and let others know we truly care about them.

Like most people, you have probably missed a chance to get to know someone and later wished you had spoken from your heart. Perhaps you assumed that the person didn't want to respond to you, and missed the ironic truth that he had the same fear about you. Perhaps he held back, worried that if you saw him too clearly you might not want to know him.

Often all it takes to let go of such a fear is to make up your mind that you *are* going to connect with someone in a mutually fulfilling way. Say to yourself, "I want to interact with at least one person today in a way that leaves both of us with a feeling of deep satisfaction."

Even if you only say, "Hello, how are you?" the intention to connect will be carried in your words. The other person may not respond openly, but you will know the feeling of having created an opening for something to happen.

Call to mind a person you would like to get to know better. Choose what kind of relationship you want to have.

Each time you make the effort to connect with one person, it will become easier to do so with others. You will quickly discover that your capacity for friendship is much larger than you thought.

1. Think of a time when someone came up to you clearly intending to offer you friendship. How were you able to recognize his or her sincerity? Did you feel a response within to his or her words, voice,

or gestures? Was it something about his or her smile or eyes that spoke beyond the words and acknowledged you as an equal and valuable being?

2. How have you responded to this invitation in the past? Think of specific examples.

3. Imagine in detail how you would like to respond in the future. Be specific.

4. Think of someone with whom you would enjoy a friendship. Imagine the mutual delight that the friendship would bring. Get a sense of how your voice would sound as you began to speak. When this image is clear in your mind, call the person and set a place and time to meet together. When you meet, speak openly and honestly of your interest and appreciation.

CHAPTER 18

Beyond Fate: Weaving a New Future

Many people think their lives are controlled by fate and destiny. On the one hand they see fate as a course of events—usually bad—predetermined by an irrational and impersonal outside force. On the other they consider destiny an unalterable course of events that brings them good fortune. By believing in a set future, they can avoid taking responsibility for expanding or enriching the ways they give and receive love. They sigh and say, "That's just the way I am," hoping their friends and family will respond by expanding *their* compassion and understanding.

If you think it is your fate to struggle for acceptance, or to be lonely, then of course it will be. Your beliefs make it so. Rather than think of your relationships as set by either fate or destiny, consider what would happen if you believed that your experiences with other people were created entirely by you.

Try thinking of your life as a magnificent tapestry, and yourself as the weaver. Imagine your relationships as patterns in your tapestry, woven not by fate but by your own hand, and according to your own visions. You —and no one else—have the power to add new patterns, and to unravel and reweave old ones with yarns of a finer quality, forever bringing in new colors and designs.

If you don't recognize and use this power to weave your own future, you will continue endlessly repeating the patterns you learned in child-hood. Your ways of relating will become rigid and your roles set, making your future predictable and unfulfilling.

Even if your parents were models of mutual acceptance and apprecia-tion, their patterns are not necessarily like yours. You can now weave your own unique patterns that express more fully who you are. Merely by stepping back and looking over the last decade you will see how you have already rewoven patterns that *could* have been your "fate." When you were younger perhaps you sulked and resorted to one-word re-sponses when others attempted to communicate with you. ("Is anything wrong?" "Nope." "Are you sure I haven't done anything?" "Yep.") You probably changed that pattern by selecting one you liked better. As soon as you realized you weren't bound by fate to retain the childhood one, it was easy to unravel.

The best way to establish a new pattern is to practice it with everyone, not just selected friends. Once you replace an old automatic reaction with a well-chosen new response, everyone around you is affected. Even casual friendships and chance encounters with strangers will have more meaning.

The more people you can bring into your life and experience a deep caring for, the more beauty you can weave into your future. As you get to know new friends, you can adapt their unique patterns and interweave them with your own; each will highlight or add texture to the others. Gradually, you will weave a tapestry of great beauty and original design to set off your unique humor with compassion, your spontaneity with focused commitment, and your clarity with openness to adventure and delight.

1. Select one unsatisfactory pattern that has seemed like your fate, and think about what you would like in its place. Give the new pattern a name (love, truthfulness, patience, clarity, beauty).

2. Surround yourself with books, pictures, poetry, and music that remind you of your chosen pattern. Put the name of the pattern or symbols for it on your mirror, your refrigerator door, by your bed, on the dash of your car.

3. When you see the reminder, reflect on every way you can imagine to weave this pattern. Be specific about where you can express it next. Find new opportunities. Don't just try to achieve it—consciously act as if you already have it. Every time you do, you will be weaving another thread of the pattern into your tapestry.

CHAPTER 19

Beyond Ambivalence: Acting on Deeper Commitments

Some people say ambivalence is like sitting on a fence. I think it's more like constantly jumping back and forth from one side of the fence to the other.

Ambivalence swings us back and forth between wanting and not wanting something. We may spend a few minutes or several years in conflict over such dilemmas as accepting or rejecting a job offer, or choosing whether to marry, to stay married, or to have a child. A woman with two small children may fluctuate between wanting a divorce and hoping for a closer, more loving relationship with her husband.

We are usually comfortable with the levels of connecting in our relationships, so long as they are consistent and familiar. But when we see hints that a relationship could be much more fulfilling, our discomfort grows. We gingerly reach out, then pull back again. Like turtles, we may spend more time inside our shells than we spend looking around to see where we are going.

When we can't decide between two alternatives, it's often because two important sides of us have different ideas about how to improve our lives. Neither side may have the best solution. When one side wants to do something and another does not, the struggle consumes energy, usually much more than we realize. At its most intense, ambivalence can use up almost all of our energy.

One side of you may fear doing the wrong thing. You will hear yourself thinking, "I hope I don't make a mistake." If this happens, take a few moments to look at the fear. Comfort your fearful self; be understanding. Rather than let fear obscure your vision, look at the decision from the perspective of the overall life direction you desire.

Everyone has watched a child on a swing slow down until she can step off onto firm ground. To slow down your swing of ambivalence, all you have to do is relax and let it happen. The bouncing from one choice to another will slow and then stop, and you will be able to gently step off.

In the stillness that follows, you will be able to choose with clarity.

Once your emotions are calmed, you can look more closely at the direction of your life. We each have a path to follow that will enable us to love life and embrace it wholeheartedly. I call it the path of joy. To live our lives to the fullest we must each make a personal commitment to follow our highest path. We find it one step at a time. The first step to finding yours is to make a list of your deepest desires. Once you have a clear idea of what you want for yourself, you will begin to see that where you once thought you must make an either-or decision, you actually have many more alternatives to choose from. You are free from the forced feeling of an either-or decision in which neither alternative feels vitalizing. You will find it easier to act on your deeper commitments and select the choices in all relationships that support those commitments.

You will feel more than relief each time you make a decision that embraces life; you will feel your energy level rise as you move confidently toward your personal goals. Individual decisions may seem like small steps, but upon your small choices rest larger ones. Many people have made a major shift in their lives by making one seemingly "small" choice.

1. Take 5 minutes to make a list of your deepest desires. Call them life goals, ideals, or purpose. Then take 10 more minutes to combine, add to, and refine them before listing the major ones again on a new sheet of paper in order of importance.

2. Think of a situation in your life right now that involves other people, and about which you are ambivalent. It could involve spending more time with your family, getting in or out of a relationship, setting up a business partnership, and so forth.

3. In the light of your direction in life and your most important desires, what new choices appear? Imagine the immediate effects of each choice. What effects can you imagine will happen at least 3 years in your future?

CHAPTER 20

Beyond Hope and Fear: Taking Action However Small

To love and to be loved, not only now but always, is a hope shared by almost everyone. In our own ways, we're all trying to turn our hopes into realities; the stronger the hope, the more we try. But just saying the words "I hope" implies that we don't feel we have the power to make our hope a reality. Since we don't know how to make it happen, we begin to fear that it won't. The hope and the fear, soon reach equal intensity: one a positive and the other a negative expectation.

When we hope that a relationship can be more joyful and fulfilling but have an equal fear that it can't be, we feel stymied. Not knowing what to do, we may fear doing anything at all. This inaction can be wise, because anything we do out of fear rarely gives us what we hope for.

If you have begun to look for a way to get beyond the duality of hope and fear, you are already on your way. You can separate who you are from the part of you that is experiencing a lack of power. It often helps to hold a pillow or a child's teddy bear in front of you, and let it represent the fearful part of you. Imagine that you are speaking to it lovingly, as you would speak to a frightened child. Ask precisely what its fear is based on. Give this part of yourself a new and larger perspective; help it to see the entire picture of your situation. Show it other sides of you that are there to assist, since no one side can possibly carry all the responsibility. Then give it a long hug of appreciation for how hard it has tried to keep you safe and out of danger, in spite of its limited perception.

This communication with the fearful part of yourself is one of the most important connections you can make. As you listen to, appreciate, and teach it, it will respond from its desire to assist you. And it will begin to see more clearly how to make your hopes become realities.

Once your fear has been calmed, you are more free to choose action that is appropriate. You can be daring, innovative, even ingenious. Begin with a very small step. Any action, however small, will start the process of transforming your hope into a belief. The difference is enormous between "I hope I can find someone who will love me" and "I believe I'll be in a fulfilling relationship soon." Put your energy and thoughts on the probability of success instead of on a vague possibility, and you will always see another step to take. Each action, though it may seem small in itself, gives you a broader sense of confidence and power.

Until you do take action of some kind toward each of your hopes, you will find that the alternating focus between hope and fear uses up your energy. Instead of remaining in this polarity, make the picture of each of your hopes as precise as possible. Often all you need is the encouragement to take a step. The best thing to do is join a group that gives its members support for their hopes. If you don't know of such a group, form one. Three or more people who meet regularly not only have a great deal of fun together, they have the pleasure of seeing the successful results of their positive focus and encouragement. Your group can use this book as a source. After a few sessions spent practicing the exercises at the end of the chapter together, each of you will see yourselves with a new focus of compassion and appreciation and will find your friendships increasing in number and in depth of connection.

1. Select a special pillow or stuffed animal to represent the fearful side of you that is opposing a hope. Speak to it. Become aware of how hard it has tried. Appreciate it. Teach it new ways to help you.

2. Select one small step that will help make your hope turn into reality. Mark on your calendar the date and the time you will carry out that step. When you've done it, decide on the next step or two and mark those on your calendar. Make sure you set aside the time to do them.

3. Continue to communicate and to make a real connection with your fearful side, particularly if you feel hesitant to take new steps toward your hope. Expect a rush of energy and confidence as this side begins to use its natural abilities to assist you, uninhibited by its old fears.

CHAPTER 21

Beyond Restlessness: Carrying Out the Intention to Connect

Whenever we are restless, we burn energy without anything to show for it. Restlessness is a signal that something is wrong, and it's a signal worth paying attention to. If we ignore it, we become impatient, then irritated, and finally, angry. Sometimes we blame other people. Paradoxically, the antidote to restlessness is not patience. Attempting to be patient will actually increase your impatience. However, by intensifying your discomfort, it may move you more quickly into action.

Restlessness creeps over us when we spend time with people in ways that are not satisfying. We always have a choice about how to use our time, so long as we are willing to accept responsibility for the consequences (good and bad) of making that choice.

In conversation we all become restless when others speak automatically, without putting their whole selves into their words. You may try to hide your feelings in the belief that your friends won't suspect your restlessness. But people always know when someone feels impatient with them. Both of you will suffer until one acknowledges the loss of connection. You will also lose your sense of connection by going along with someone else's interests when they do not overlap with your own.

The minute you feel restless when you're with someone, say what you are feeling. "It sounded like a good idea to go with you to hunt bullfrogs at midnight, but I feel so restless sitting here that I am feeling a wave of anger coming over me." You can assure your companion that he or she has not done anything *to you,* but that you now realize you want to look at other options for spending your time and energy.

If you feel restless even when you are alone, take a close look at how you might use your energy more effectively. Until you redirect that energy, you will feel as if you are stepping on your car's accelerator with the gears in neutral—you're using a lot of gas without going anywhere.

If you are impatient with your life in general, think about what *does* feel important to you. If you put your energy into something you truly value, your restlessness will disappear. No one around you need change, even though you may have thought that some of them should.

When you turn your attention to areas in which your interests overlap with others', you will make new connections with groups. If a group project intrigues you, yet you become restless in meetings, see how you can get the group to connect on a deeper level. Until it does, effective action is not likely to happen. Group connections are natural when the members focus on a shared vision that is valuable to each one. Use the energy you now express as restlessness or impatience to act with courage, confidence, and power to offer a solid connection to a group, a friend, or your mate.

1. Whenever you feel restless or impatient with others, consider it a useful signal. Think about how you can use your abundant energy to do something for which you do feel enthusiasm.
2. If you belong to a group that seems to have bogged down, think about what action you could take to bring it to life again.
3. Plan your strategy (each chapter in this book suggests ways); watch for the appropriate moment (such as during or immediately after an informal group break); and speak up.

CHAPTER 22

Beyond Assertiveness: Acting from Genuine Power

We assert ourselves in order to gain what we believe is fair. Sometimes it works, especially when we are confident and assured rather than aggressive and dogmatic. When it doesn't work we find ourselves caught in a power struggle, because our partner (mate, client, boss) is equally strong-minded about her or his position. If neither party backs down, the conflict quickly escalates out of all proportion to the situation. Often our struggle in the relationship continues long after the issue is settled.

There is another way to get what you want. Imagine that you are on one side of a river and want to cross over to the other side. When you feel headstrong and assertive, the way across is like a precarious rope bridge. You may get across, but you will have to struggle to keep your footing. If you are also uncertain and ambivalent, the ropes sway back and forth. Instead, you can connect with your inner strength—the genuine power in all of us. Then you will see a graceful, steady bridge across the river. You simply walk across.

Three steps will get you from assertiveness to genuine power. First, state your assertion clearly: "I want and deserve more money (fewer hours, a transfer, more territory, less stress) in my job." Second, state what you think you will gain if you get the change you want: "I'll know *they* value and appreciate what I am doing." Third, focus on the larger issue that lies behind the specific one: "What I really want is a job that I believe in and enjoy." The resulting clarity will enable you to choose what to do.

When we use assertiveness, we zero in on an "unjust" situation and claim or demand a specific thing or change from someone. When we act from genuine power, however, we see the situation more clearly and can state a preference, suggest another way, or offer to continue—*when* we can find a way to bring joy and meaning back into it. If your housemate leaves clothes over every chair, or gets a cat you are allergic to, you can stop and use your imagination. Imagine what your relationship would be if you got her to change, and see if *that* is what you really want. There's no need to use a cat as an excuse to make changes if the issue is really greater. Power comes from the awareness that we always have free choice.

You have used that power countless times all through your life. You may have forgotten those times, because when we act with genuine power we don't even notice the changes we bring about. We say or do only what seems obvious.

When you express your genuine power, you identify with your true self. See yourself now as a member of a group of people who are using increasing levels of power and are intent on using it wisely. Focus on the wise use of your power in the areas where you do have it rather than on those where you don't.

What works best to bring joy and creativity into this relationship? How can you use your power to gain trust and cooperation for this group's work? When you ask these questions before taking action, you will walk to the other side of the river on your graceful, stable bridge of power.

1. Think of one area that offers you a minor challenge and tempts you to be assertive in order to make a change.
2. As a person with genuine power, how would you act in that situation?
3. Practice your new role as a powerful person. Imagine exactly how you would stand, what you would say, and how you would feel inside as you spoke. Continue to practice—in front of a mirror or role-playing with a friend—until you feel your genuine power to act in specific situations. You may wish to choose a guide from among the spiritual leaders throughout the ages whom you can call on to assist you to use your power wisely.

CHAPTER 23

Beyond Deserving: Moving with Trust and Intention

Imagine that you are at the seashore watching a woman stand with out-spread arms, waiting for the waves to wash over her. But she is standing too far from the water and the waves cannot reach her. She is puzzled because other people are enjoying the waves, when she deserves them as much as they. Now, imagine gently taking her by the hand and leading her into the water. Like that woman, to get what you want and believe you deserve you have only to put yourself in its path and let it wash over you.

Think of one particular kind of relationship you have felt you deserved for a long time and yet do not have. Have you perhaps been looking the other way when that relationship was actually within your reach? Have you met an attractive person and had the urge to call, but decided not to? Have you been introduced to an executive, personnel director, or banker, and yet hesitated to suggest a working relationship? Has your brother or sister warmly offered to assist you, but you modestly de-murred, saying you were doing fine by yourself?

When you begin to recognize the limitations you have imposed on yourself in the past, try mentally replaying each situation. Rewrite your script from the point of view that you deserve only fulfilling, creative connections. As you do this, you will create your future, for our futures are merely a continuation of the feeling we have about our past. You cannot change the past event itself, but if you relive and rescript your memories, you will free yourself to create in the future your newly envi-sioned past.

The process may sound magical, but it works because you step out of your pattern of hoping and into a pattern of moving with trust into what you know is waiting for you. Besides, you understand much more now than you did then; each experience has made you wiser.

People who talk a lot about deserving new or more joyful, expansive relationships usually doubt that they truly deserve them. What we are sure we deserve, we simply open ourselves to receive. If we want more friends who are loving, and we know we offer an equal exchange of compassionate caring to them, we soon find people in our daily lives who fit our desires.

Our ability to create relationships and enjoy each more fully expands throughout our lives. Every experience we have in which we reach out and truly connect with another human being adds confidence, understanding, and strength to our next interaction. This is true even though we have felt frustration or disappointment in past relationships.

Each time you connect with another person, you have a new opportunity to give and receive love in some form. It's up to you to realize how much you deserve and to be willing to receive it. Rather than believe you have to work hard to deserve more, you need only to look around and see how much better your ability to connect with others is today than it was six months ago, and then to imagine that proportion added to your ability six months from now. Trust the power of your expanding warmth and love; your ability to move toward those you truly care about will continue to multiply as long as you live.

1. List several kinds of enjoyable relationships you have now. Include people you see often and those you see rarely, friends you know well and acquaintances you know casually. If you don't know all of their names, simply write "the lady at the supermarket counter" or the "ice cream man."
2. Go over this list to see how much you deserve and already have because of your intention to connect and your trust that you can do it.
3. Add the kinds of new relationships you desire to this list—a hiking companion, a fellow vegetarian, a joyful questioning child, a traveling companion. Keep the list by your kitchen stove. When you read it each morning, imagine yourself having a wonderful time with each of these new companions.

CHAPTER 24

Beyond Struggle and Effort: Allowing Playfulness

Imagine watching a man and a small child trying out snow skis for the first time. With sweat on his brow, the man struggles hard to hold his balance. When he falls, he hits the snow as if it were a solid sheet of ice. The child tumbles more often, yet it's clear that she likes being down almost as much as she likes being on her feet. Within an hour the child is barreling down the hill with an enormous grin on her face, while the man is still struggling doggedly, determined to learn how to ski "right." His face is stern with determination, his movements stiff and awkward.

The major difference is that the child is unafraid and has no expectations. She's simply playing; the man is struggling to achieve. The man thinks that when he learns how to ski he will relax, but until he changes his approach he will struggle to get off the beginners' run and onto the intermediate runs. Once there he will struggle harder to push himself onto the advanced runs, never able to enjoy the delight of skiing.

Like the determined skier, most of us have struggled to relate with love to others and have doggedly begun again after each discouragement. This struggle is like an endless battle to gain what one part of ourselves doesn't truly believe we deserve. We can break free by changing that belief. If we believe it's all right to get what we want, without struggle, we can gracefully accept our natural abilities and playfully expand our resources. Composed and self-assured, we can learn to love like the little child learns to ski—delighted in our discoveries when we fall and delighted when we are on our feet again. Enjoyment comes easily when we see everything as our chosen play. (After all, each of us is free to choose another game any time we wish, so long as we cheerfully take responsibility for the consequences.)

The first step to ending struggle is to recognize that struggle always needs something to push against, and usually that something is our own fear. Those facets of our personalities that do not yet have as much light as other parts are easily overcome by fear. To stop their struggle we have to calm their fear. Think of each fearful part of yourself as a child left alone in the dark, isolated from all the fun and action going on outside his door. When the child cries, you can simply walk into his room, turn the lights on, and let him participate in the fun. After only a moment of sniffling, he is content.

In the same spirit, take these fearful parts into the light, and give them new roles to play. Let them have fun too. If they are struggling, for instance, because they fear you can't meet a deadline from your boss, show each one how to help you do the necessary work with humor and delight.

You can calm them simply by taking time to play, to laugh, even to laugh at yourself struggling, to step aside from the drama of struggle and see what you are learning from a new perspective.

If you have a coworker who turns out the same work you do playfully and with serene confidence, learn from this person. If you have no role models in your present or your past, create one in your mind—one who laughs, enjoys relating to coworkers, works steadily and creatively.

People who work with pleasure and confidence have calmed the sides of themselves that believe in struggle. Your own struggle and effort will diminish as you think about this new role for yourself. Tense minds and tense bodies constrict expansive thinking. Laughter clears our minds and bodies of tension and expands our natural poised productivity.

If you don't feel like laughing, experiment with laughing anyway—for five minutes. At first it will be phony, then interesting, and finally real. You will be laughing at your feeble attempts to laugh—and at your resistance to doing it. The ideas that form in your head while you are laughing originate in your heart. Respect them. The ideas that spring from your high spirits are the most alive for you. And if they are alive for you, they will be alive for others. They can show you the way to play productively with anyone you "work" with.

Still, being "productive" and finding relief from struggle in humor is only one step on your path to success. Laughter will be a natural part of everything you do, not just an antidote, when you eliminate the belief that struggle is necessary for success in any of your relationships.

1. Make a list of skills that you express with natural poise (organization, patience, gaining cooperation from others, encouraging others, logic). You may be so unconscious of these skills that a friend will have to assist you.

2. Rehearse a new way to relate. Think of a particular struggle you are having with someone in your life right now. If you were told by an eminent physician that you would not survive any more struggles,

how would you solve the conflict? Would humor work? Would compassion help?

3. If you are still having trouble, imagine that the life-endangered patient is your best friend. What suggestions would you make? Now follow your suggestions.

Part IV

SPEAKING AND LISTENING WITH INTEGRITY

CHAPTER 25

Beyond Feeling Shy or Hesitant: Enjoying Self-Expression

Imagine a coat of freshly fallen snow covering mountains and valleys. This soft blanket protects the land until spring draws green stems upward. Until then, the snow protects the seeds, allowing them to germinate at the appropriate time and establish roots before the buds appear.

Shyness about expressing yourself is like a blanket of snow protecting germinating thoughts. Yet they will burst through effortlessly when the time is right. If you hesitate to express your real self, perhaps it is because you feel the need for further exploration. Instead of regarding yourself as shy, and perhaps becoming self-critical, notice how *all of us* hesitate to express ourselves honestly.

We are all afraid of being hurt. As a result, we develop ways to protect ourselves from being seen too clearly, from being misunderstood or made to look foolish. Practice watching and listening for each person's true self behind the facade. Respond to that part; you need do no more than simply smile and nod while you look him straight in the eye. You will intuitively know the right moment to speak, for you will sense his openness to listen.

Everyone has had the experience of feeling hesitant to join in a conversation. Keep asking yourself what level of communication you would really like. You don't have to be satisfied with small talk. Wait until you feel you can contribute, and trust your ability to engage in an exchange you really enjoy. Your desire to participate will be conveyed through the tone of your voice, your inflections, and the pauses between your words, and people will respond. It is the feeling behind the words, not the subject of conversation, that gives the most satisfaction in personal connections.

Express yourself with enjoyment; your passion for life will be obvious as you speak, and that passion will draw others into your experience. Even the shyest among us have talked with enthusiasm many times, perhaps with a small child, a friend, a partner, a grandparent. When you recall those times you will open wider the door to expressing yourself in the future. When you say directly what you know or believe, your words will have an impact on everyone who listens. When you express the fullness of who you are, you will encourage others to do the same.

1. Think back to the last moment when you expressed yourself fully and felt the wisdom in your own words.

2. Just before this happened, what were you thinking? What image of yourself were you seeing? How did you feel the connection happen —suddenly, or gently and gradually?

3. Imagine that you were watching yourself from a distance. Picture your posture and your face as you spoke; remember what the other people said as they responded to you. Hear again the sound of your words and of theirs. Remembering and reexperiencing these moments of self-expression will help open the door to expressing your true self again.

CHAPTER 26

Beyond Delaying or Avoiding: Expressing Honest Responses

A small child with a splinter in his finger avoids the inevitable sewing needle, even though we adults can see how easy it will be to remove the splinter once he volunteers to hold his finger out. The same applies to any emotional splinter, such as an unresolved conflict with a friend that is causing pain. The longer we delay, the more we become accustomed to the splinter—we even miss it when it is no longer there.

When we feel uncomfortable with someone else, we often delay acknowledging it. The prospect of saying we're uneasy can evoke more anxiety than whatever made us uneasy in the first place. Once we've decided the splinter needs removing, the process is quite simple. Rather than taking the blame or accusing the other person, we have simply to state in what way we feel uncomfortable.

Although anyone who has used this method knows how well it works, most of us still avoid it. The reason is fear—fear that we will lose something valuable, such as the other person's "love" or their company, even the entire relationship. Yet when feelings are withheld, silent messages are nevertheless being sent and received; as a result, both people have an uncomfortable feeling of distance. No matter how cheerful we attempt to act when together, we share a feeling of separation rather than closeness.

A struggle for power is often at the root of the problem. Such a struggle immediately takes both people away from their hearts and pulls them into a contest of wills. If you find that someone has drawn you into this kind of struggle, tell him or her how you are feeling. Quite likely he or she feels the same way. Suggest that you both will feel better if you look at the conflict from a perspective of mutual understanding and compassion.

The same techniques that help you deal with minor upsets work on the larger issues as well. Take anger, for example. Without defending your reaction, you can tell the other person that you feel angry and acknowledge that you are sometimes supersensitive. The more specific you can be about what your anger feels like, the better. If you get a hard knot in the pit of your stomach, or feel incredibly tired, say so. If you put off expressing your feelings, you will soon begin avoiding each other and your relationship will fade.

When you know that you need to speak up and you don't, it is like seeing snails in your garden and letting them eat their way through your flowers. At any one moment the snails' damage is small, but as days go by the life of the flowers ebbs away.

As soon as you communicate your angry feeling, its intensity lessens. Remember, though, that expressing a feeling is different from going back over the situation that caused it and shoving in extra splinters.

Once a feeling is acknowledged, free of blame or guilt, a very interesting process takes place. Another feeling may surprise you as the old one dissolves. After anger, you may feel deep appreciation. Feelings of dissatisfaction are often replaced by emotional warmth that acts as balm to your wounds and validates your true worth.

1. If you have avoided expressing your honest response to someone, ask yourself what is the worst thing that could happen if you did. Then weigh that against the consequences of continuing to avoid the issue. If the price of avoidance seems high and a positive result seems possible, make an appointment to meet. Look the person in the eye and express yourself honestly, gently, clearly. Many positive feelings that have been covered up by the negative ones may come from this exchange.

2. Think of specific people in whose presence you feel valuable, who stimulate in you a compassionate feeling for yourself and for others. Plan time with these people and notice your honest responses when you are together.

CHAPTER 27

Beyond Persuasion: Offering and Inviting

The "gentle art of persuasion" is something we all use when we want friends or customers to come around to our way of thinking—usually, because we think we know something that would be good for them, or for us. But when we convince people to do something, we deprive them of the chance to take full responsibility for their choices.

The alternative to persuasion is simply to offer or invite. As soon as we sense that someone is trying to persuade us, we become cautious, even suspicious. But there is power in an open invitation. When someone freely invites us somewhere and we can see they have no *need* for us to accept, we are pleased. We may not accept the offer, but it makes us feel good to have been invited. Direct invitations bring out the best in everyone.

We can move from persuading to inviting by connecting with our own wiser selves. The more we concentrate on choosing our actions according to our own wisdom, the more naturally we will find ourselves inviting others to enjoy the freedom of their wisest choices. Few words need to be spoken for these invitations; we may not even realize we're issuing them. But the people around us will respond with renewed cooperation.

We all respond most openly when we are with people who take joy in life and enter into each new activity with genuine enthusiasm. Even if we were blind we would hear the spirit in their voices; and were we deaf, we would nonetheless sense the joy in their presence. Sincere invitations to share in the joy of life itself are irresistible to all of us.

1. When you decide to invite rather than persuade, first set up an appropriate time with your partner. Make it clear that you are issuing an invitation, not a disguised threat.
2. Notice the difference in your feelings when you offer or invite instead of trying to persuade. You won't say: "I think this would be a good thing for you to do." "You would enjoy it; you should do it."

"If you do this, it would make my life easier." Instead, you'll say: "I want to invite you to join me in ———." "This is what I see is possible; ———." "I see ——— (this result) if we work together."

Be as clear and direct as you can. If your partner hesitates, continue to give him your attention for a couple of minutes. After that, if he doesn't respond, offer to meet the next day at a specific time. Express your appreciation that he is taking time to think your invitation over.

When you meet the next day, listen carefully. If he does not accept your invitation, find out exactly what part he does not like. Without feeling hurt or defensive, suggest that he issue an invitation to you that will bring out the best in the relationship for both of you.

CHAPTER 28

Beyond "Hearing": Listening with Alert Compassion

"I can't go with you." These seemingly straightforward words can conceal many meanings. If you listen to the words alone, it is easy to misinterpret what is being said. But when you are alert to the tone, you will hear the real message: "I don't think you really want me," from someone who is hoping to be persuaded; "You asked others first," from someone who is disappointed; "I don't really want to go with you," from someone who is trying to be tactful. When you listen in a spirit of compassion, of true caring, you can connect with your son or daughter, mate or friend, on a deeper level. Your response can be appropriate, not only to the statement, but to the feeling behind it. With the genuine assurance of acceptance, you can ask your hesitant friend if there is anything you can do to make it possible for him to go with you; you can emphasize to your disappointed daughter how important she is to you.

Compassionate listening has two components: the head and the heart. Both are valuable; but either, by itself, is incomplete. "Head" knowledge alone becomes cold and distancing, compassion alone can turn into empty sentiment. By combining wisdom with compassion, however, you can reach and be reached deep within. Imagine you have a ten-year-old son, and he tells you that he is the smallest member of his class. With your head you may start looking for ways to help him grow, explain individual spurts of growth, or point out that size is not related to value as a human being. Using your compassion, you may hold him in your arms for a moment and tell him you have an idea how it must feel to be the smallest. Either approach alone is excellent; the two together are dynamite. First allow your compassion to reach out from one human being to another, then bring in the wisdom of your wider experience. Use every example you can to allow him to see his intrinsic value to you and to the world just as he is. In this way you reach out to him from a deeper level, and heal the fear that lurks behind his words.

To fix in your mind the difference between superficial hearing and compassionate listening, remember an occasion when you spoke to people who listened with complete attention to your message, to learn from you and to discover more of who you are. They didn't see you as the person you were yesterday or a month ago; instead they released past images of who you were and discovered you anew. This kind of listening is one of the greatest gifts that anyone can give. Recall precisely how you felt when someone listened to you in this way, no matter how briefly or how long ago. Then think of times when you, too, listened with alert compassion and thus enhanced another person's ability to speak with integrity.

As you develop your ability to listen with alert compassion, new thoughts and ideas will surface. You will begin to experience parts of you that are not usually involved in ordinary conversation. You will have the extraordinary experience of seeing your son, father, friend, or mate as if for the first time, beyond all the images you have held. And you will feel the love between you deepen.

1. Think of a time when you "heard" someone only with your head, then think of another occasion when you "listened" only with your heart. Get a sense of the difference.

2. Recall the first occasion, and add the sensation of listening with your heart. You will gradually feel a new level of clarity.

3. Now do the reverse: Add your head wisdom to the occasion when you listened only with your heart. Again, notice the power of the combination.

4. Recall a situation that is likely to occur again, in which you wish to listen with openness to discovery. As the other person speaks, imagine pausing to give both your heart and your head time to look beyond the words. This brief silence will allow you to reach past the hopes or fears being expressed to the deeper truth behind the words.

5. Practice this way of listening with your heart as often as possible when you are calm, so you will have the poise to do so even when your emotions are stormy.

CHAPTER 29

Beyond Swallowing Back Feelings: Expressing Yourself Clearly

We swallow back all kinds of feelings—happy ones, sad ones, loving ones, and angry ones. Sometimes this is appropriate; if by expressing them we would blame the other person, it's best to delay. Often we are so successful at pushing back what we are feeling that we don't even realize we have done so. Once we can acknowledge the feelings passing through us, without blame, it's time to express them.

To become more aware of moments when you swallow back feelings, begin to observe the act of swallowing while you are engaged in a conversation. At first it will seem as if you simply needed to swallow. However, if you observe more closely, you will discover that there is something you wanted to say and decided not to. By catching yourself as you swallow, you can examine what is being said, and what is not being said. If you wait until later to think about it, the unspoken message may be too far out of reach to retrieve.

One night an uncomfortable silence arose in the midst of a conversation between two close friends, during which the man noticed the woman swallowing. He asked what she was swallowing about. At first she insisted that she simply needed to swallow. Then she swallowed again, even though she was desperately trying not to. The more she resisted acknowledging what was bothering her, the more forcefully she found herself swallowing. Suddenly, she realized she was swallowing back deep feelings of love and appreciation that she didn't feel comfortable expressing.

Physiological explanations are not necessary for us to realize that we swallow *instead* of saying what is in our hearts and minds. We swallow rather than express our anger; we swallow to hold back our love. The tenor of our emotions doesn't matter. Some theories hold that our throats are the center of our creative expressiveness and, when we block expression, we do so literally, by closing our throats in a swallow.

Most of our lives swallowed-back feelings have gone unnoticed. Still, our bodies get stiff when too many swallowed-back feelings stack up. Some people eat too much food as a substitute for expressing themselves. They open the throat, but put food in rather than let feelings out. Others go through periods of not being able to swallow at all. (If I open my throat to swallow this food, who knows what awful feelings might come out?)

Notice that when you are in a comfortable conversation, you don't need to swallow. If you begin to catch yourself and others swallowing as you talk, approach the matter lightly, even humorously. You will find you can enjoy the process of discovering what "fearful thing" you felt the need to push back.

When you notice yourself swallowing, make a mental note of what is going on, then deal with it as soon as possible. Even better, say "Oh, I just swallowed back something—let's see if we can find what it was." Your partner may be amazed, but will probably be happy to help you discover the stimulus. By acknowledging the feeling, you will clear both the air and the tensions in your body.

Fear, even several fears stacked together, lessens rapidly as it is acknowledged and discussed without any sense of blame or guilt. If you feel embarrassed, threatened, fearful, or any of the other lively emotions you believe unacceptable, acknowledging them may seem like a big step. Yet one statement such as "A part of me is afraid of something, and I want to know what it is" releases you to share both positive and negative feelings that have been held back.

Imagine that your fears are like a small child whom you are training to become a beautiful adult. You can train that part of you that is fearful to cooperate with your overall purpose. Once you know that it is possible to speak up without harming others and still express yourself honestly, you will find it easier to do so.

We have all been open and truthful many times, even when the truth was uncomfortable. Recall a relationship in which you felt free to speak up. You will realize that you already have the skills to express yourself clearly and honestly. All you need to do is transfer those skills to *all* of the important people in your life.

1. Think of a person with whom you recently felt uncomfortable. Imagine what you could have said and didn't. In your mind, say those sentences now.

2. If you notice a need to swallow when you are thinking of one of those sentences, you have reproduced a swallowing-back reaction just by thinking about expressing yourself with honesty. Notice how it feels so that you can observe a similar feeling in actual conversation.

3. Think of a recent occasion when you spoke honestly, expressed yourself clearly, and did it with confidence and grace. Replay in your mind the response of the person who was listening. Feel the pleasure of eliciting that response.
4. Imagine speaking in the same manner to one of the people you thought about in the first step. Keep in mind that it is possible to express love and fear, compassion and cautious feelings, in ways that heal and thus make whole all of your relationships.

CHAPTER 30

Beyond Being Articulate: Speaking from Innate Wisdom

Eloquence can be beautiful, but fluent language by itself does not guarantee that words will reach past the surface of anyone's mind. If a person speaks in clever words and poetic phrases that leave you untouched, how can you respond?

If you are afraid to move beyond clever conversation for fear of being misunderstood, remember how refreshed you have felt when someone else spoke profoundly. People naturally applaud the person who speaks with true insight.

If you speak simply and clearly from your own wisdom, instead of speaking about something you've read or have been told, you will stimulate others to respond from their own wisdom. Ideas will suddenly become clear to you in response to thoughts others express, and you will find yourself saying things you have never thought of before. Whether your conversation is humorous or serious, simple words are always best. The higher the level of wisdom you reach, the more straightforward your words.

Learn to listen, especially during animated conversations. Wise observations often get lost in the excitement when everyone wants to talk and there are no real listeners. Make it a point to respond to what others are saying. When you are talking with just one other person, pause to think before you speak. The change of pace will help to open a new level of communication.

Practice with a friend. If you resist making quick replies, you'll be able to go beyond automatic responses. As you pause, you'll find that several responses will run through your mind. Each succeeding response comes from a deeper level of your wisdom. When you do speak, you will often be surprised at what you say. That's because your ability to see behind what is being spoken grows as you develop the courage to pause and listen to the voice within you before you speak.

1. Agree with a friend that you will each pause for about 30 seconds before you respond to one another. Pay attention to the responses that enter your mind. As their pace slackens, choose the one that is the most exciting to you. This exercise will quickly lead both of you past the original conversation to one that is on a much deeper level.
2. After practicing with a good friend, you will be able to pause gracefully even with the people you don't know well. Try this with a variety of people. Notice the new directions your conversations take.

CHAPTER 31

Beyond Embarrassment: Speaking Out with Honesty

Do you think you're too short? Too tall? Too young? Too old? Whatever you are silently embarrassed about will block you from connecting fully with others. We all get embarrassed when we fear we have been foolish, awkward, or dumb. Usually we haven't been any of these things. Embarrassment is almost always based on our exaggeration of an imagined shortcoming or something harmless, silly, or totally natural that we've done—or are afraid we might do.

Imagine that your embarrassment is an Alka Seltzer tablet, much too big to swallow. See yourself drop it in a glass of water; watch it fizz and gradually disappear. When you confess an embarrassment that you have carefully hidden, it fizzles out in just the same way.

Take a moment to look at some of your images of yourself. You may have been taught not to speak about money or strong feelings, not to cry in front of someone, not to acknowledge that you enjoy running or skipping, or chasing sea gulls on the beach. If embarrassment keeps you from doing any of these things, ask yourself who would disapprove. Is that person with you now? If not, go ahead and enjoy yourself.

To free yourself from limiting self-images you must first acknowledge your embarrassment. Then speak out honestly about the "foolish" thing you want to do. Your friends probably won't think it's foolish at all.

Awkwardness often arises in close relationships when we suspect we have said or done something wrong and are embarrassed. The only way out is to be courageous and acknowledge the situation. When you tell what happened, it will probably sound funny—even to you. It's hard at first to admit, "I'm afraid I just put my foot in my mouth," but once you do you'll quickly discover the difference even a flash of openness can make. Most companions respond with a sigh of relief and soon begin to share, with gales of laughter, their own fears that have turned into embarrassments.

You don't have to wait until you are hemmed in by embarrassments.

Choose an important person in your life right now and make a list of the things that embarrass you when you are with that person. You can even rank the intensity of your embarrassment on a scale from 1 to 10. Include everything you can think of. Then read the list to that person. Many of your items will sound funny as you read them aloud ("my long neck, my short legs, my foreign-sounding name"), and they'll sound even funnier when your partner admits he's embarrassed about the opposite (his short neck, long legs, ordinary name).

The simple act of speaking out honestly is refreshing to both people. It's like raising the shades and opening the windows to air out your house. After you've read the items on your list, you will discover that you can talk about them together with ease. And you will find a new vitality in your relationship. Not having to hold anything out of sight leaves both hands free to reach out with loving appreciation.

1. Make a list of small embarrassments—subjects or activities about which you have been inhibited or which you have avoided altogether. In each case, add the name of the person who stimulates this embarrassment. Develop a simple code no one else will understand so you don't feel the need to censor this "embarrassing" list. Then put down the whole truth.

2. Begin with the name that appears most frequently. Imagine saying to this person precisely what you feel uncomfortable about when you're together. You can preface your acknowledgment by saying that it may seem very strange to someone else, but that one part of you is embarrassed that you are not taller, thinner, younger or older —even richer, smarter, braver. Try this with each name on the list.

3. If you cannot imagine being able to acknowledge to the people on your list the feelings that have blocked a satisfying relationship, then invite a close friend to come over and "sit in" for the other friends, listening without responding while you speak. Practice will make it much easier to speak with the actual person, but don't be surprised if your original embarrassment has simply fizzled out, along with the need to speak of it again.

CHAPTER 32

Beyond Words: Communicating in Silence

Have you ever tried to converse with someone who had laryngitis? After a few strained attempts to talk, she probably gave up and simply listened quietly as you spoke. In the silence, you had an opportunity to hear yourself in ways that are not possible in normal conversation. If you have ever spoken aloud to yourself on a deserted beach, or in the woods, you have experienced the power of silence as a response to your words.

If you want to know who another person really is—and, in turn, be known to the other person—sit together in silence and gently connect with your eyes. You will communicate without speaking a word. You can feel the kind of warmth you feel when you silently watch a tiny baby, a sleeping friend, or a child who loves you. If you remain totally present, not daydreaming about the future or reflecting on the past, you will feel as if a veil is being lifted—a veil that is usually held in place by words. This veil has separated you from your ability to be with, understand, and accept another person completely. Every time you practice being with another person in silence, without the words or gestures, you will become more comfortable with this deep level of communication.

Each of us is a sending and receiving station. We send and receive all sorts of silent messages and emotions all day long. When our minds are stilled and our emotions calmed, we expand our ability to receive and embrace the love between us. In silence you can feel the power of love to join with a small child, your mate, your grandmother. The more people you learn to fully accept and love in silent communication, the more aware you become of your enormous capacity to love.

Words cannot fully express the depth of who you are; nor can they transmit a full measure of caring toward someone else. When words, even eloquent words, flow too rapidly, we all stop listening. It is as if we feel we must defend ourselves from receiving too much verbal information without the time to assimilate it. But when we alternate speech with comfortable pauses, we can look deeply within ourselves and see the larger vision of who we are. The *pauses* between our words carry much of our true meaning.

When you share silence, you can touch the other person's essence with your own. And though you may rarely see that person, you will always remember the heartfelt connection made possible by silence.

1. Find a friend with whom you truly desire to communicate in silence. It may be anyone who enjoys adventure.

2. Agree to experiment with the power of silent communication. For brief periods of time (4 or 5 minutes) remain silent, yet totally aware of being together. Sit facing each other, make eye contact, and allow your natural feelings to flow. Notice when your mind wanders back to yourself (What is my friend thinking? He seems to be looking at my nose; I wonder if I look old to him.) or to outside things (I must get to the store to pick up some eggs and bread . . .).

3. Afterward, talk to each other about the things that went through your mind. Laugh together about how fast your mind moved even as you tried to still it.

4. Observe how much closer you feel as you resume your usual patterns together. See if you feel more loved and more loving, more accepted and embraced.

Part V

ENJOYING FREEDOM AND ABUNDANCE

CHAPTER 33

Beyond Fear and Caution: Opening to Adventure

A tiny fawn, guarded by his mother, learns from her what kinds of creatures to stay away from. As the fawn grows up he learns to avoid threats to his well-being. As small children we heard our parents say, "Be careful. Don't talk to strangers." When we were children we didn't have enough experience to discriminate correctly. Their warnings were appropriate, meant to keep us safe.

As adults, we can discriminate between people we would like to know and those we want to avoid. But often we find ourselves held back by fear and caution.

Trust your intuition as you reach out to others. You can find the people in any gathering who carry the natural scent of goodwill. You may need a few minutes to get a sense of each one, but once you think about it, you can do it. As you honor this inner knowing, you will grow even more sensitive to it, and it will enable you to connect confidently. The more sure of your intuition you become, the more you open to new adventures and friendships.

When you approach a new acquaintance you may feel as cautious as if you were entering a foreign country. Your heart may beat fast, your breath become short. These are the symptoms of fear, but they are also the signs of adventure. Remember how you felt just before you jumped off a diving board for the first time, or at the start of an exciting race? Once you got into the adventure of diving or racing, the symptoms went away and you were delighted with yourself. The same thing happens when we have cautious, fearful feelings about connecting with new people, or about deepening a familiar connection.

By renaming these feelings and going straight into the experience, you can pass beyond any fear and hesitation. You can turn "be careful" fears into anticipation of "exciting adventure" just by renaming your feelings.

1. Review a few of the outstanding times in your life when you did reach out spontaneously to someone and were richly rewarded.

2. Think of one person with whom you have felt too fearful or cautious to be yourself. What might happen if you could truly connect with that person? What would happen next? Keep asking yourself, letting each answer supply the next question. For example, "If I were to connect more fully with my husband, I might expose too much and then get hurt. If I did get hurt, then I would be even more cautious about revealing too much of myself again. And if I became even more cautious, I would probably be very guarded every time I spoke to him. And if I became more guarded with him, I would gradually become more guarded with everyone I know. And if that happened I would feel imprisoned within myself and probably have a hard time communicating honestly with everyone I know."

3. After your cautious and fearful side has responded to your questions, check with your true self to see whether you believe these fears are realistic. Now you have a much clearer idea of what has been holding you back from connecting with people in a spirit of adventure. All you need is a willingness to examine your fears, and you will begin to shift away from caution.

CHAPTER 34

Beyond Possessiveness: Assuring Mutual Freedom

If someone offered you a chance to own a star in the heavens, you'd probably laugh. The idea of possessing or owning another person is just as absurd as pretending to own a star. We may join with others out of our own freedom of choice, but we cannot possess or be possessed by anyone else. Believing someone has a right to your time and energy is pretending that she or he can own your life energy. Freely offering your time and attention is a gesture of love. There is a great difference between the two.

Do you feel you need to get permission from a mate to be with friends you enjoy, spend a weekend alone, sign up for a class on sailing? If so, your mate is probably in the same constricted position of having to ask permission for any new ventures. Spouses who ask each other's permission, rather than acting on their own inherent freedom, can easily become entangled in mutual control through permissions withheld. The result is blame and guilt.

Imagine that you will be given a very unusual gift for one day—the gift of total freedom. Act today as if you were free of the urge to be owned by, or to own, another person. Perhaps you have believed that you owe it to another person to spend every evening together. This evening you are absolutely free to choose the activity that will bring you the highest joy. You may decide to sing with a group of friends, to attend a concert, or simply to sit all evening in the public library poring over articles about a subject that interests you. It may increase your joy to invite your partner along. It isn't what you do that's important, but that you choose it freely.

You may never before have experienced this kind of freedom for an entire day, but there's no reason for you not to enjoy it. First decide that you want to feel that you are fully expressing who you are. Once you do, you will find ways to assure the people around you that they too are free.

Try it out for just a day. During the other six days of the week, allow yourself to continue relating to your family and friends in your usual way. If a day seems too long to experiment with freedom, try it for an hour.

In that hour you are free to think, say, and do whatever you wish. Ask yourself what you most deeply want. Try on each answer in your mind to see how much inner satisfaction and fulfillment it promises to give you.

If you have children, free your children for an hour or a day. Tell them about your experience of taking responsibility for your own freedom. Assure them you will protect their freedom and, instead of reacting to them with judgments or defensiveness, that you will listen with an open mind. Offer this also to your mate, mother, father, and friends.

The illusion that we need permission to express our own human spirit is like molasses underfoot. The stickiness doesn't stop us completely, but it slows our steps. Pulling free is exhilarating. Eventually, you may choose to start every morning with a commitment to freedom—to create, to initiate new ideas, and to respond freely to others. Doing this costs nothing; freedom is available to everyone who has the courage to try it.

Silently or aloud, invite the people around you to accept their inherent freedom. You will rediscover the creative spark in one another. As your own enjoyment is reflected by others, you will mirror that joy and thus redouble your vitality.

1. To let go of possessiveness and gain mutual freedom, write letters to everyone by whom you have felt owned, telling them how good it feels to be aware of your freedom and theirs. Do not mail the letters yet. On your next day of experimenting with your freedom, read the letters again. Add to or subtract from them for clarity, and then imagine what would happen if you did mail them, or if you spoke directly to these people. Would they find an inner relief at not being possessed? Would your words inspire them to discover new ways of connecting with you that assured their freedom and yours? If so, mail the letters. If not, write the letters again until you are satisfied that they are truly a gift to yourself and to the others.

2. Imagine what it would be like to be in charge, even briefly, of your own free self—of your time, body, mind, and emotions. Feel the pressure lift. Think about what you will be doing once you enjoy this freedom, with whom you will be connecting, and how and what you will be creating in the world.

3. When you are satisfied that you have reclaimed your freedom for one day a week, add another day, and then another. Breathe in your sense of freedom each morning upon awakening. The more deeply you breathe, the more deeply you will experience your free self.

CHAPTER 35

Beyond Hero Worship: Appreciating Your Inherent Qualities

Each of us has some traits that are in full blossom and others that are in the process of opening up. We tend to take for granted the attributes we have already developed, saying, "Anybody can do that." The qualities that we are just beginning to develop are the ones we tend not to see. As they stir within us, we start to notice them—but we see them in others rather than in ourselves. Thus we first experience our new qualities by admiring them in other people. Often, admiration leads to hero worship. Hero worship—admiring someone who exhibits a quality we think we don't have—separates us both from the person we admire and from our developing inner qualities as well.

When we designate someone as "special," we often forget to separate the person who is expressing the quality we admire from the trait itself. If we admire a person who is surrounded by loyal friends, for example, we see all the love she is receiving, but we often miss seeing the attributes that make her loved. When we do notice a quality in her, it is one that we also have in some stage of development. For example, you might admire her listening abilities. At the same time I might be attracted to her flexibility. A third person might admire her humor and wit. The woman surrounded by friends would be expressing all three traits, but each of us would focus on the quality that is developing within us.

Each of our heroes acts as a mirror to show us our own unrecognized strengths. Each of us sees our own image, yet we believe we are looking through a clear glass.

Often, neither person realizes what is going on. In a relationship, the game of hero and admirer is nearly always an unconscious conspiracy. Once someone has accepted the role of hero, however, that person is not likely to give it up. If you are the admirer, breaking out of the game is up to you. The hero is equally trapped, but is less likely to acknowledge it.

When you admire another person, recognize that the qualities you appreciate in her are also in you. This realization will lead you away from unnecessary "humbleness" and toward a true humility, rooted in a sense of the potential you share.

We never need to stand at the fence of other people's yards and long for the peaches hanging on their trees when our own are laden with succulent fruit. Acknowledging each quality that is inside of you encourages its development; the new qualities you develop will add to your life as well as the lives of those around you. Your quality of humor, for example, stimulates your family's sense of humor.

Your goal, of course, is not to have other people regard you as a hero. That would only put them in the position you have just escaped. Instead, encourage others to recognize their own inner qualities. If they hesitate, you can point out to them what is obvious to you—that they have within them, in some stage of development, the very quality they are admiring in someone else.

Every time you discover a new positive trait and begin to express it, you become a much more interesting and exciting person to be with. You will even enjoy yourself more. We have all looked at ourselves in the mirror and admired the reflection. You will appreciate the beauty of your own qualities once you recognize them within yourself. When you see the same qualities in someone else, it will then give you added pleasure and delight, because you know that you share them.

The next time you start to make someone your hero, stop and say to yourself, "She and I have a wonderful trait in common. I can learn from her how to develop mine and express it even more fully."

1. Today, set aside 5 or 10 minutes, without interruption, and think of a trait or quality you have admired in another person. Allow yourself to realize the truth and beauty of that same quality within yourself.
2. Imagine expressing this quality in a variety of ways, and imagine the response in others. Every time you use your imagination in this way, it becomes more natural to express your love, strength, courage, humor, and honesty in the world.

CHAPTER 36

Beyond Seriousness: Experiencing Lightness and Humor

When we take ourselves too seriously, we cut ourselves off from the most enjoyable moments of our lives. We turn our focus inward, and feel burdened by obligations and commitments. Such seriousness keeps us from experiencing the joy of lightness and humor, even in "play." Look at the faces of joggers, couples eating dinner in restaurants, vacationers waiting for flights to Hawaii. How serious so many of them look, and how boring.

The kind of seriousness that is valuable to us does not make us feel somber and dragged down with duties; it is clearly focused on what is truly important in our lives and motivates us to get it. Lightness and humor are a natural part of this kind of seriousness. The areas of our lives where seriousness is appropriate, such as expanding our love, compassion, and understanding, often slide by unnoticed. Yet we take seriously the situations that will make little difference a year from now. We can learn to see the humor in these natural dramas of life if we simply reinterpret their meaning.

We can decide which side of ourselves we want to express in any situation. How? By catching ourselves at the very instant we begin to interpret what is happening. We may think events have an inherent meaning, yet we have all felt indignant one day and genuinely amused another day by the same thing; the difference was in how we interpreted the situation. For example, your mother thinks you could run your life better and tells you so. You can either interpret her position with amused appreciation, knowing that she means well, or as a serious imposition on your independence. When you feel good humored you can laugh at the omelette that turns into scrambled eggs, and serve it with a flourish as a mark of your creative individuality.

We each have a light and humorous side just waiting for the chance to step in and add delight to our relationships. Such a spirit evokes genuine smiles of amusement and laughter. Laughter is the bridge to intimacy. It dissolves barriers and reconnects us with those we love. When we laugh we release the same tension as when we cry—but laughing is more fun.

Rather than laugh at someone else in order to raise our self-esteem, we can laugh at the incredible human predicament we share. We are all in the same boat, full of fears and wishes, wanting to be loved (or at least appreciated) by people who are important to us, and to give the love that surges in our hearts.

When you feel absolutely free to play, you enter into the fun with high energy and spontaneous enthusiasm. That spirit is ever-present in you. To find your humor and bring it forward, imagine that you are observing a conflict between your serious side and your light and humorous side, as an amused adult might watch her two children building a sandcastle on the beach. As the waves come to wash it away, one moans for help while the other laughs with delight. They are both reacting to the same situation; the only difference is in their interpretation. We go through many dramas in our relationships with our children, our families, our friends and coworkers. Each one can be seen as serious or light, depending on *our* interpretation.

When you see yourself with humor, you energize not only yourself, but your friends as well. They feel free to see their light, joyous sides. Think of what you can give to all your friends once you have it yourself—the gift of a lighthearted spirit.

1. For the rest of this week, imagine yourself gently smiling at any serious efforts to say the "right" thing or act the "right" way toward people around you, at efforts not to rock the boat or look foolish in any way. Imagine yourself expressing your lighthearted self. Stand up in the boat just for the fun of it, and acknowledge the delightful frailties of being human.

2. Look at your list of things to do for the day. Invite your light, spontaneous side to examine each task and suggest new approaches to it.

3. Practice interpreting minor annoyances with your lighter side. As you enjoy the new habit, confidently insert the new pattern of humor into more "serious" occasions.

CHAPTER 37

Beyond Obligation: Living from Free Choice

Some people live out their lives in a mire of obligation. Their connections are based on indebtedness. They compulsively count favors—not just favors, but sizes, flavors, and categories of favors. All of us have experienced the difference between acting from obligation, and acting from a sense of delight, joy, giving freely. For example, feeling obligated to speak up in a meeting depletes our energy, whereas we fully enjoy and are energized by *choosing* to speak out.

The ordinary events of our day repeatedly offer us the choice to feel obligated or to respond freely. Our thoughts set the tone for everything we do from the moment we awaken, open our eyes, and put our feet on the floor. You'll make an enormous difference in your whole day when, instead of thinking, "Another day of having to meet my obligations, (going to work, calling my clients, paying my bills)," you think, "Another day of choosing to act on my commitments—because I *want* to." Acting out of obligation is exhausting. Living from free choice is joyful. It speeds up the day, yet expands time when we need it.

Some people might say, "But isn't that selfish?" These people don't realize that you can freely choose to give. Whether of your time, energy, or material things, freely given gifts are far more precious than gifts given out of obligation. If you have ever been successful in manipulating or pressuring someone to give to you out of obligation, you know how unsatisfying that can be.

"But," some say, "can I avoid obligation? Is it possible to have a life without it?" No one can make us feel obligated. We do it all by ourselves. Others can nudge us with reminders, sighs, and outright demands, but only we make obligations real.

Phone calls, dates, appointments, meetings, and social events can soon fill up all your time. And your time is your life. Who really enjoys being taken out to dinner or given presents by someone who feels obligated to do so? In such situations we can't express sincere feelings, so we talk with effort about nothing, or stare in silence at our hands, our forks, or the television screen.

How much better to respond freely to life, choosing what to do, pulled by your own inner vision instead of pushed by someone else's. When you choose freely, you may take the same action that used to feel like obligation, but you will be doing it now because you want to.

Freedom can only follow from the realization that it is possible. From that realization you will be able to take steps to handle your genuine commitments. In any situation begin by acknowledging to yourself and your companion what you *are* willing to do out of genuine desire and delight—positive commitment—rather than what you don't want to do out of obligation—which might be called negative commitment. It's never too late to take this step—or too early.

Next, take initiative for changing the tone of relationships that have drifted into obligation. (A sign that you have slipped into obligation is the presence of guilt, discomfort, or pressure.) Then describe what *would* make that connection joyful.

Perhaps you may feel tempted to try living by choice. It's not possible to live freely if your world is based on obligations. You can't blithely live a life of choice if you hold other people obliged to you. But you can enliven every connection if you respect and insist on mutual free choice. As you release yourself you will inevitably release your friends. Since all obligation is from the past—even though often from the unexamined past—tell each person you want to consider the score even on both sides.

How long would you like to be obligated for something you did in the past? One year? Five years? A lifetime? Start with a clean slate by mutual agreement. Create a new style of relating with each important person in your life that fits *both* people's purpose.

Your free will is much more generous than your sense of obligation. Try responding freely for 8 hours and note the changes in your energy level, your enthusiasm, your ability to get things done. Compare it with 8 hours of living out of obligation. Then try choosing freely for a week and watch your renewed interest carry you toward your highest vision for your life.

1. How would your life be different if you were not obligated to people close to you, and if they were not obligated to you?
2. Make believe for a moment that you are no longer living out of obligation to anyone. See yourself awakening tomorrow morning with a feeling of free choice. Assume that you choose to continue the connection with those closest to you, but with the understanding

that neither of you is obligated to each other. What choices would you make?

3. Free others of obligation to you. Encourage them to live this one day freely from moment to moment, choosing that which has the greatest meaning and purpose to them.

CHAPTER 38

Beyond Jealousy: Releasing with a Blessing

Struggling with jealousy is like falling into white-water rapids. You're smashed against the rocks, sucked under by the currents. You pop up, gasping for breath, only to be sucked under again. Caught in a whirlpool, you're out of control. Your only chance is to go limp, and let the force of the current shoot you to the surface.

Like the first splash of icy water, jealousy is a master awakener. Regardless of the anguish—or perhaps precisely because of it—struggling with jealousy precipitates powerful changes. *Continuing* to struggle, however, is like being caught in a whirlpool. Your thoughts can hold you in the circular current of jealousy indefinitely—if you struggle for control of someone else's choices. The way out is to let go of all illusions of control. Then you are free. You open your eyes and see the blue sky again.

Jealousy has many emotional components: fear, anger, hurt, rage, and a few other lively emotions in rapid succession. These emotions become more or less intense depending on how you interpret the situation. When you feel jealousy coming over you, identify the specific emotion and rate its intensity. Use a scale of 1 to 10—1 being vaguely annoyed and 10 being a wish for the person to fall into a cage of hungry tigers. When the intensity lessens, observe more closely the thought you have just had.

You control jealousy by the power of your imagination. If you decide someone else is more valuable (more beautiful, more desirable) than you, jealousy pops up. Once it's controlling your emotions, every comparison will escalate your feeling of not being good enough.

You can counteract this by playing the "what if" game. Start by purposely making interpretations that lower the intensity of your jealousy. For example, your friend has the job you want. Imagine you can actually see into the future, and know that in six months you will have a job that seems like creative play, all because someone else got the job you *thought* you wanted. Everything depends on your creative imagination. Many of my clients, overwhelmed by jealousy when their professional positions were given to someone else, have been surprised at the "what if" game. When they engaged their imaginations, they let go of jealousy and became intrigued with their creative ideas. In less than three months, they usually called me to announce their new jobs—and sheepishly admitted how much more satisfaction they had found.

Anyone who stops trying to control another's choices and, instead, takes control of his own imagination, can move through jealousy like a raft on the river. You'll find it natural to release with a blessing, whether a job or a relationship, when you see the benefits to be gained from your ride through the rapids.

1. Recall an episode that once stimulated your jealousy.
2. What did you gain as an extra benefit in your life? Do you now share more of your feelings or reach out with more compassion to others? Are you stronger, more independent? Do you have a deeper trust in your intuition?
3. If there is any jealousy in your life now—even a touch—play the "what if" game.
4. Instead of pacing the floor with your surge of extra energy, try an experiment. Begin building something you want—a tool shed, shelf, planter box—and as you hammer in each nail, feel your power to create with mind and body.

CHAPTER 39

Beyond Need: Accepting Innate Abundance

Once we have a roof over our heads, food in our stomachs, and a few clothes on our backs, our basic life needs are filled. Most of us can provide these things for ourselves. In addition, however, we all want to feel loved, cheered, humored, encouraged, cherished. And we are often tempted to define these as needs that can only be gotten from someone else.

Ironically, when we define something as a *need* we make it much more difficult to get. Have you ever noticed how much more easily and quickly your desires in a relationship are filled than your "needs"? If you are wondering why, think of the people who have "needed" more reassurance from you and of how reluctantly, if at all, you gave it.

All of us pull away from the pressure to fill other people's imagined "needs" (for more love, more security, more help). The idea that we are "needed" may give us pleasure for about one week. After that we may perceive the needy person as an imposition, and gradually grow to resent his or her demands. Once you agree on some level to be indispensable to someone else, that person acquires a staggering measure of control. You can soon be overwhelmed. Even the thought of withdrawing the help makes you feel guilty that another's "needs" are not being met.

The more people who consider you indispensable, the more demands you will have on your time and energy. You might temporarily avoid becoming resentful because you feel good about serving others, but eventually you will feel imposed upon. You will always be expected to be available to handle difficulties for friends and acquaintances. In the midst of all of this neediness you will eventually have no time to pursue your own life, and your available energy will be drained away. If you continually set yourself up as being needed, you will soon be needed by so many people that their demands will become impossible to meet. (For some chronic "helpers" this is the only cure.)

Why not start weaning the people who are pressuring you with their "needs"? Show them how to fill their perceived needs from their *own* inner riches. Point out to them that what they think they need is already within them. When your friend "needs" to be told that you love him reassure him that you do, but focus on how much love you see in him. When he "needs" to be forgiven, offer forgiveness, then tell him how forgiving he is, using specific examples. Soon, he will learn to accept and enjoy his own unlimited stores of loving compassion.

After they learn how to accept their innate abundance, friends who once "needed" you may simply enjoy *being* with you. Two people who accept each other's innate abundance can have wonderful times together. No demands are made, no expectations are set up.

Knowing your own abundant spirit of love will affect every relationship. People intuitively respond to you in proportion to your acceptance of this abundance. Have you ever noticed that when your life is overflowing with friends and with fulfilling time alone, it seems as if everyone you meet wants to know you better?

As you open and expand from within, you will indeed delight in the company of kindred spirits, but you will no longer feel that you "need" them. Nor will you credit anyone's claim to "need" you. Knowing your own abundance will free you to delight in real connections, and leave all others free to reach out to you from the strength of their abundance.

1. What needs do you have that you hope someone will fill?
2. How would your life be different if you could fill some of them from your own innate abundance? What would result from that change? For example, "If I didn't need someone to tell me I am wonderful, I would not be so eager to please or to pretend feelings that I do not have." Or, "If I could know without a doubt that I am an inherently loving person, I could reach out with love more easily."
3. Imagine that you're watching a movie of yourself enjoying many fine friendships with friends, family, coworkers. Add a soundtrack to your movie so that you can hear what is being said as you watch. Now step into the movie and feel delight and humor, warmth and caring, in each connection.

CHAPTER 40

Beyond Control: Affirming Autonomy

Have you ever met anyone who was worried about being *too* controlling? Neither have I. Most of us are more likely to feel that others are controlling us—getting us to do things their way.

If you feel controlled by someone, you can't connect with that person from your heart. Once the issue of control gets started, it begins to permeate every area of the relationship—even determining who orders the meals at a restaurant. Feeling controlled does have its good points —it can provoke us into deciding what *we* really want. Once we begin to explore the possibilities, we can become intrigued with the idea that we are free to choose for ourselves—in large issues as well as small ones— and discover how many equally fine ways there are to relate with love.

The only way you can feel free to love anyone (including your parents, siblings, children, marriage partner) is to assume that you are free to choose independently, using all the knowledge and experience you have. Resuming your autonomy feels like a gentle waterfall flowing over your body. Although often denied or forgotten, the almost heady feeling of freedom has always been yours. But you're the only one who can claim it.

Control is actually an illusion, for we have to *agree* to play the game of being controlled. After all, we may complain that someone tells us what to do, *but we have to follow that person for the game of control to work.* No one can make us follow. If someone for whom you have little respect gave you a command or attempted to manipulate you, you would simply yawn and ignore him.

If you learn to exercise free choice in minor situations with your family, you will enjoy natural autonomy in the big choices as well—deciding from your own wisdom how to spend money, whether to rent or buy a house, how much to spend on a car, on education, on recreation.

In partnerships, major choices (moving to another city, changing life-styles, choosing to have children) call for partners to accept each other's autonomy. Trading off (you control this issue and I'll control that one) is fine if it works. But consciously choosing in the light of your own desires and your partner's desires on each issue will bring you closer. As soon as you are willing to fully recognize the autonomy of your partner in every issue, you will fully affirm your own.

One of the last forms of control most of us give up is our attempt to control the actions of other people. We all have times when we want others to do things our way. Who has not stood in the voting booth and wished he could control his friend in the next booth who is canceling his every vote?

Most tempting of all is to control other people's happiness. We sometimes push to get their moods to match ours—"Can't you smile a little?" "Aren't you going to say anything?" "What are you thinking about now?" As a result, they defend their moods even more strongly.

In the end, no matter how much energy we expend trying, we cannot control others. But *affirming your mutual freedom* draws you closer to each person you care about, And leaves both of you free to interact in a warm, compassionate spirit. As you release even the desire to control others, you will exult in your own autonomy. You will feel as if a weight has been lifted from your shoulders. As you delight in taking full responsibility for your choices, you will form friendships with others who also enjoy being responsible for their independence—who rejoice in awakening to the power of compassionate autonomy.

1. Identify an area in your life where you feel controlled—economically, politically, professionally, recreationally, emotionally, intellectually. Even if you have played only a small part in allowing that control, identify the part where you silently gave permission by going along with it.
2. Recall or imagine someone who honored your freedom to be yourself. Imagine hearing his or her voice again, seeing the light in his or her eyes, feeling the touch of his or her hand on your shoulder.
3. Now imagine that person encouraging you to affirm your autonomy in the area from step 1 where you felt controlled. Affirm that you are autonomous in every decision, and silently endorse the freedom of others as you meet them.

Part VI

CONNECTING WITH COMPASSION

CHAPTER 41

Beyond Right and Wrong: Recognizing the Wisdom of the Heart

Each of us has an inherent wisdom that can guide us in everything we do. It can burst forth unexpectedly, as the blossoms come on a tulip tree before any leaves have unfolded. Imagine that the wisdom of your heart is about to blossom, enabling you to listen to your family and friends with a new openness.

Acting from wisdom transcends being either right or wrong. We all like the feeling of being right, but when we find ourselves driven by a need to *prove* we are right we get caught up in trying to prove other people wrong. If we insist we are right and want others to agree, the frame around the conversation becomes too small; it only leaves room for one of us. Even if we win and prove we are right, we lose, because we are left alone.

Sometimes we express our need to be right by talking too much. At other times—and this is worse—we are so convinced we are right that we remain silent, nodding and attempting to appear tolerant of others' viewpoints while our minds secretly remain closed.

Whether expressed or unexpressed, the *need* to be right leads away from satisfying connections rather than toward them. You can convince everyone at your table that you know the right wine to order, but you may end up drinking it with dispirited friends. Connections with our friends have a way of disappearing when we insist on proving we are right.

The need to be right surfaces when other people touch an area of our lives that has a fear attached to it—the fear that if another position were right, it would somehow make our position wrong. Any belief we hold dear—from the best way to raise children to what is worth spending time or money on—can make us feel vulnerable. Feeling "touchy" is a clue to fear; the more fear, the more adamantly we tend to defend our "rightness," afraid that if we are wrong our image will be tarnished.

If you hear yourself justifying or defending your statements, stop for a moment and look at the situation. Are you pushing your point out of fear of being wrong, or are you really discussing a subject of interest to the group? If your friends are being responsive, nodding and listening to you with open minds, go ahead. If not, ask yourself if the point is really important. Drop your approach if you see that it doesn't make any real difference to the group, and wait for a better opportunity to present your view. Acknowledge your realization by saying, "Somehow it seemed important for me to be right about that." Resist giving a reason.

Then, without saying anything else, begin breathing more slowly and deeply. After several deep breaths most people begin to relax and find that a serene feeling comes over them. It becomes easier to focus on the larger picture. In your imagination, see the point you were trying to prove as a log floating down a river, moving past where you are standing and out of sight. Freed from fear and tension, your natural wisdom will have a chance to emerge. You will see the value in all beliefs; each has a germ of truth, including yours. What you say will seem like common sense and will begin to connect you with other people. With practice, you will learn to catch yourself before you dive into a passionate monologue or shake your head to interrupt someone you think is wrong. You'll be able to stop and smile, contributing wisdom rather than engaging in a contest to prove right or wrong.

When you are with friends or your life partner, you can have enjoyable times unspoiled by disputes. If tension arises over where to go or what to do, turn the conversation away from who is right and who is wrong. Talk instead about what you want to get out of being together. Be very precise; describe the picture in your mind of what you *do* want—not what you don't want—from your time together. As you talk, you'll feel more calm, and from that feeling new thoughts will spring. As you speak in a simple and straightforward manner, you may think you are only stating the obvious. But watch your partner's face closely as you speak, and you will see a change. As you both open all your channels of perception, the atmosphere will clear and the tension will dissolve.

1. The next time you are with one or more friends, take a few minutes to talk about what you want to get out of being together before any issues of right and wrong have a chance to come up. Each of you will have an idea. Once you agree, establish how each of you will know when you have achieved your goal. If your goal is to enjoy yourselves and have a good time, find out what the common denominator is. Once that has been agreed upon, whatever actual activity the group engages in will be enjoyable. If you and your partner want inspiration for a special project together and also to experience a loving afternoon, you can have both. There is no one right way to

bring forth inspiration or to express love. When you both have a harmonious purpose, you will each initiate ways to create what you want together.

2. If, in a conversation with friends, an issue of who is right comes up, find the larger purpose you share in common. If, for instance, your ideas about family or world peace are not embraced by the others, focus on the fact that each of you wants and values peace. Find out what peace actually means to each person. Get each to describe his or her most recent individual experience of true peace. With this kind of focus, questions of right and wrong don't emerge. Each of you can move past familiar answers and speak from true wisdom.

CHAPTER 42

Beyond Being Reasonable: Knowing the Ways of the Heart

Being reasonable is an excellent quality. As you learn to reason well, you function much more efficiently. The *habit* of reason, however, may become so comfortable and familiar that you forget about the discoveries of the heart that lie beyond reason.

It may not be reasonable to drive half a day to spend 3 fun-filled hours bicycling in a beautiful valley, but the heart knows its true value. Only through heart-knowing do we grow strawberries for the delight of eating them off the vine, when reason alone would tell us they cost twice as much to grow as to buy in a store. If we combine reasonableness with heart-knowing, we can choose precisely how and with whom we spend our time.

You may not realize it, but you already know how to see from the heart. When you feel a deep appreciation of someone, your heart has been touched. Reason may say that nothing has changed, yet suddenly you perceive the person differently. When you experience moments of joy with someone, you feel a sense of wondrous appreciation for her just for being who she is.

Seeing with the heart leads to a different level of understanding than reasonableness alone would allow. It enables us, for example, to reach out with compassion to someone we don't know. It allows us to communicate warmth with something as simple as a hand on the shoulder of a lonely or discouraged fellow traveler in distress.

Continue to appreciate your skills at being reasonable, but begin at the same time to listen to the wisdom of your heart. Learn to move freely into the space that lies outside the enclosure in which you normally live, no matter how large this enclosure may seem. Being reasonable, we may spend all our time with the same group of people; the vision of the heart leads to connections with a wider range of people. Every person with whom you come into contact—the man on the street corner who sells newspapers, the president of your company—offers you the opportunity to discover a gate that opens into a larger life. On any given day you can choose one of the many gates available to you and walk through it.

1. Choose one personal connection in which you have already explored the boundaries of reasonableness and in which you would enjoy going beyond these boundaries. Children are often the best gates through a boundary, because they are not yet caught up in the restrictions of using only reason. Start with a natural and easy connection.

2. Imagine how you would feel if someone were to act as a gate for you to go from reason to the wisdom of your heart. In response to this opportunity, you may want to offer to serve as a gate to help that person make a similar transition. Age, sex, background, and relationship do not matter.

3. Take time tomorrow (or today) to get on eye level with one child you know and invite him to share in an unreasonable but totally delightful adventure with you. It can be as simple as mirror writing together, breaking into an old penny bank of yours and buying ice cream, or sending off balloons with messages inside.

4. You may be fortunate enough to know an adult who still loves to play and laugh. Spend time with that person in order to learn more about expressing yourself from the heart.

CHAPTER 43

Beyond Having Things in Common: Sharing the Ability to Envision

We need more than things in common to make real connections with our new acquaintances or with friends or family. When we limit our exchanges to discussion of shared schools, friends, sports, careers, or gourmet tastes, we may miss making a true connection. I call such exchanges "sleep-talking"; we speak and respond from habit, without being really awake or caring. We soon get bored or restless because neither person knows how to get beyond the small talk.

Every real connection we make requires a spontaneous leap from where we are to an unknown place. We can't plan or plot it out. We have to make the jump without stopping to think. In one moment we decide, and bound over the surface differences that have kept us apart. One woman described an extreme example of how she made this leap:

"I was standing on a downtown curb at night waiting for my bus when a dirty, rather disheveled man came shuffling by me, pushing a shopping cart. He looked at me and mumbled, 'Are you married?' I started to turn away, but then I decided to respond. After a couple of polite exchanges, I asked, 'Are *you* married?' He burst into tears, saying his family had been killed in a car wreck. A part of me said, 'Watch out, you don't know this man and he's dirty.' But in that moment I simply reached out and put my arms around him and held him. He had lost his path in life. Something within me opened up to experience our common humanity. I knew I was taking a risk, but it was as if I had suddenly awakened from my ordinary and somewhat mundane thoughts and feelings. We were both nourished in a very real way and as my bus pulled up, he tried to give me the only possession he had, an apple."

Not all of us are able to bridge a gap so wide. But we can all make real connections that reach into the core of our common humanity, connections that touch and transform us. Unless we feel more expanded and compassionate or more aware of ourselves when we meet people, we have not made the kind of connection that affects us in any substantial measure.

We have all turned away from someone because we couldn't find anything in common. But what we see as big differences between ourselves and someone else are insignificant in the context of our common humanity. When you offer a true connection, people know the difference. Be willing to enter a conversation wanting nothing for yourself. Have no expectations, no scenario in your head of what you want to happen. If you do have one, fears of failure or rejection can interfere. The other person will pick up your intention and react to that, and the spontaneity between you will be lost.

When you make a real effort to reach out to someone, your guard is down. You forget to hunt for things in common; you forget about yourself. You don't try to manipulate the situation or the person. You lose all self-consciousness. And then it happens.

Your genuine interest in the unique way this person expresses his humanity draws him out. His response often surprises both of you. If you each remain open to this connection, you both feel a desire to give to one another. Honor that desire. Give everything you can. Every gift—a smile, a flower, a treasured idea—expands your joy when it is given to honor your common humanity.

If you want to create more occasions for connecting, sit in the sun, take a walk, or sit in front of a fire with another person. Express whatever you are feeling about your own discoveries in becoming more fully human—whether that means you feel more caring, more open, more aware of your freedom, or simply that you're learning to listen to others. Honor moments of silence as much as you do speech. Brief and comfortable silences happen spontaneously when two people sit side by side. Each moment of silence invites you into your less explored, more deeply enjoyable identities. You may or may not acknowledge to each other the deeper sense of self and of each other that surfaces, but you both will feel its pleasure.

1. Think of one person with whom you would like to relate beyond the level of what you have in common. Set up a meeting with her. Tell her you have a sense of the real person she is and want to connect with her as true friends do.
2. Plan leisure time together in a new place—picnicking, walking, canoeing. Find a place away from other people where you can let go of your usual roles and just be your real selves.
3. Allow silences to happen. Do not expect the other person to speak, listen, or act in any particular way. Let yourself simply be who you are without any fixed expectations. Be willing to be surprised as you

speak about some personal discovery, some intense awareness of beauty, of sound, color, or feeling.

4. When you are alone, you can discover a deep level of compassion and understanding within yourself by recording your thoughts and feelings as you walk along the countryside or sit beside a lake. This connection with yourself will enable you to connect more easily with other people.

CHAPTER 44

Beyond Pressure to Do: Embracing Your Stillness

We each experience pressure differently: in our stomachs, in our heads, in our necks and shoulders, even in our hearts. At some level we all realize that too much pressure can be physically harmful. It can cause headaches, ulcers, back problems. It wears down the body's resistance to disease. We are often not as aware of how pressure devitalizes our spirit and diminishes our joy.

Two kinds of pressure keep us tense. One is external, the other internal. Deadlines and job commitments can create external pressures, but these are usually temporary. Internal pressures we create ourselves, and they are unending. We set up one after another. Many times they are efforts to do more of what we consider to be a "good thing." In our roles as parents, we pressure ourselves to do more for our children; in our roles as professionals, we set deadlines to learn more or earn more. With friends and family we push ourselves to pay back obligations. Many of us keep ourselves so busy with hobbies, trips, entertainment, or sports that we never experience the quiet times during which people learn to trust and love each other.

How can we move from "doing" under pressure to "being" in a peaceful state of harmony with our true selves? First, we need to know exactly what we are missing. If you were sitting on a hillside feeling a deep sense of peace, letting your mind, body, and emotions rest, and someone asked what you were doing, your first instinct would probably be to answer, "Nothing." So long as you believe that enjoying a peaceful moment alone is "nothing," you will continue to pressure yourself to always be doing "something."

The "you" that provides the life energy for everything you do is a vast spectrum of *being*. Little of it is used for *doing*, either mind-doing or physical-doing. When you release the pressure to express your being through doing, you open up to other spheres of who you really are. In these spheres you will find the compassion that releases you from the continuous round of a life of doing. When you embrace your still self you achieve a clarity that enables you to see through many illusions of busyness.

Every life can be simplified. I could probably see how to do it for yours. And you could see how to do it for mine. We both see how to do it for our friends' lives. But it is harder to know how to help ourselves. What's more, we resist advice because we fear what or who is waiting beyond our busyness. The fear runs so deep we don't think or speak of it; we simply move fast from one commitment, job, recreation to another—or, more exhausting, from one intimate partner to another. We do for other people; we do for ourselves. We do for the pleasure (or pain) of doing.

Every connection you make will give you a deeper fulfillment when you release your pressure to do and come to know who you are in your stillness.

Look to the *source* of your urge to do. If you find a fear of inner silence, sit quietly with that fear. When you feel the most pressured, you have the greatest opportunity to know your true self. Sit down, lean back, and reflect on who you are—and why you feel the need to be doing. You will be refreshed simply by asking the question, and opening to receive an awareness from within. You will feel your emotions quiet and your mind slow down. Then you can begin to enjoy the unpressured you—the relaxed you that experiences a certain mystery in the beauty of a sun ray streaming into your room without feeling the need to photograph it, to control it with window shades, to paint it, or even to describe it.

Turn inward with strength and joy, and you will find it increasingly natural to balance stillness and "being" with useful activity. How will your stillness affect your connections with your friends and family? Everyone you know will be affected in some way by your new sense of balance, for every shift you make in your life is as an unspoken invitation to other people to do the same.

1. Distinguish between your internal pressure and external pressure. The first is merciless and independent of circumstances; the second has a definite end, in response to a practical commitment.
2. Select one internal pressure that interrupts you when you want to sit quietly and simply be with your self. Ask yourself what is the point of it. Using your answer, ask what is the point of that. You can shake off internal pressures by subjecting them to self-questioning. Ask a partner to listen and help you remember your new wisdom.
3. Choose a time when you are rested and sit in a comfortable chair, alone, with your eyes closed. Open your heart to experience yourself as a loving being, without the need to do anything. If you feel the need to do something, simply jot down a note so you will remember

it, and continue to embrace yourself in stillness. Softly repeat, "I am a loving being." Feel your response as you do.

This exercise will lead to more harmony in all of your connections, for people will begin to reach out to the self you set free instead of the busy one who used to live under pressure.

CHAPTER 45

Beyond Established Roles: Engaging from the Heart

When you listen to the sound of a flute softly trilling, or to the clear notes of a violin, you are immersed in a world of sound without words. It can feel as if the notes are filling your body from the top of your head to the base of your spine with a pattern that is beyond you and yet within you. When you connect heart to heart with someone, you change your ordinary reality in much the same way.

We play different roles with each of our friends; with one we advise, with another we listen. We limit our interactions with most people to our role and their roles. As daughter to mother, we miss the woman-to-woman heart connections that we could have. Men struggle to break through their roles of being a strong man, father, protector, or sportsman to simply reach out from their hearts.

In every role we play we forget who we are. An actor can walk off the stage and resume his true identity, but we walk off of one stage and directly onto another. Each role represents a different character in the drama of our lives—we each have quite a repertoire. Everyone who knows our roles knows what to expect from us, even what we are likely to say next.

Why question our roles, especially when they give us security? Because what begins as an authentic way to express ourselves soon becomes an automatic response. The more polished and charming our roles, the more difficult it can be to step out of them. When you are playing out a role that isn't connected with your heart, your days feel flat. In contrast, you become enthusiastic and energized when you connect with others from your heart.

Don't be hard on yourself if at one moment you make the decision to be more loving and at the next moment you find yourself back in an unloving role. The will to love brings up all that is vulnerable in us for the purpose of healing.

All that stops us from just being ourselves is the fear of being seen too clearly. When you relate from the heart, you don't need to cover your true self with roles.

To engage from the heart, think of yourself primarily as a loving being and secondarily in any specific roles—doctor, lawyer, merchant, chief. Speak honestly and openly with the people around you, whoever they are. You may find yourself speaking more slowly than usual, often with no idea of what you will say next. Relax and continue. If nothing comes, enjoy the silence. Even in silence, you will feel more serene.

You can create recipes for heart-reaching through the power of your imagination. Start with the basic ingredients—abundant caring, adventure, and humor. You will invent a new recipe for each person and the result will nourish you both.

If you feel out of practice and self-conscious, borrow a friend's small child for an hour. When she looks up and asks your name, she is reaching out from her heart. Children naturally speak from their hearts, and remind us how to do it.

Words that carry the energy of the heart are healing. Remember them and let them feed your soul if you feel discouraged, sad, or lonely. Gather favorite memories of loving connections with your parents or grandparents when you were a small child, with your teachers and friends now. Each memory will nourish you and help you reproduce its good feeling in the future.

1. Think of someone you want to relate to from your open heart.
2. Now put your right hand on your own heart. Breathe deeply and easily. Hold this focus until a deep feeling of peace comes over you.
3. Let your left hand represent how you feel with that person. Place that hand under your right hand, which is over your heart. Feel your heart open to that person and your resistance in that role melt away.

CHAPTER 46

Beyond Relief: Experiencing Delight

Relief is getting your taxes in the mail on April 15, passing a difficult test or exam, not losing your job, or the departure of your long-staying houseguests. You can breathe a long sigh of relief and go back to your normal emotional baseline. But even though the worry and bad feeling are gone, you're only back to neutral on your scale of joy.

If we suddenly found relief from every problem, most of us would still find ourselves stalled in the no-man's-land between feeling spirited and spiritless. We can get rid of a disease, make an extra car payment, end an unhappy relationship, but delight does not automatically sweep over us. We simply need to change our point of view, to stop looking for ways to lessen anxiety and start sensing the value of each precious moment of life. The result will be delight.

Each relationship in life offers and invites delight. But our habit of living for relief interferes. We imagine that delight is impossible until all of our problems have been solved. Animals can live in constant danger of being captured or eaten alive, yet between chases they revel in delight with each other. It's not death we're afraid of, but looking foolish if we enjoy ourselves even though a big problem looms on our horizon. Who judges our foolishness? Not our friends—only our own over-serious sides.

Delight comes from valuing each moment of life, from asking ourselves what on earth could be so important that we let it take away our happiness. If we relish a morning walk in the sun, why do we put it off until the sun is gone? Because we are thinking, "How can I bask in the sun when my stock (car, house, business) may lose value?" If friends invite us to join them in feeding the squirrels, or enjoying the vibrant colors at sunrise, why do we decline the invitation with an excuse?

Many of us routinely refuse ourselves joy. We wouldn't think of dancing through our own homes (even alone, where no one can see us) out of delight in being alive. Delight comes from simple things—from seeing beauty and color and light, hearing melodious sounds and resonant voices of love, feeling rich textures, smelling fragrances, and tasting the fruits of the earth. Delight never depends on circumstance. Delight is marveling in the miracle of life itself and our intrinsic freedom to celebrate with love.

We need only to decide that every segment of our day is as important as any other and we can begin to celebrate the joy of being alive. Like children, we can create our own delight, even in the midst of terrible world or personal crises. Since our world is in a crisis that may last 25 years, we may as well begin to appreciate the quality of each hour we are alive and stop worrying that we may not live to be 100 years old. We can celebrate the gift of life alone and together with friends and lovers, children and parents, at any moment. If we try to solve our problems before we allow ourselves to rejoice, the moment will not come.

Take time each day to connect with your *élan vital*—your life spirit— and you will find many occasions to dance, play, sing, be outrageously lively—to watch the butterflies and hummingbirds, to smell the flowers. Take someone with you, age three to ninety-three.

1. What percentage of time do you spend seeking relief in each of your major relationships? Choose the percentage you want to spend in delight with each person—10, 30, 50, 80, or 90 percent. Do you believe it is possible?

2. Ask the other person in each relationship to choose the percentage of time he or she would like to spend in delight with you. Include your children, your parents, your friends, and any other person you spend time and energy with.

3. When you have discussed your desired levels of delight together, make statements to each other that begin, "I delight in ———. I feel enthusiastic (lively, responsive, alert, animated, adventurous, dynamic) when I ———." Do this without holding back what comes to mind. If you get an idea that you do not wish to share, simply acknowledge it by saying "censored." List each other's ideas as they flow.

4. Go over the list and see which ideas are possible now, and which you both want to set up for next week or next month. Block off days on your calendars to savor delightful times together.

CHAPTER 47

Beyond Proving: Knowing from Within

If you feel the need to prove something, you are not yet sure of it. You don't try to prove that the sun is shining when you walk outside into its warmth. Neither do you feel the need to prove to anyone the qualities you are certain of in yourself.

If you feel compelled to prove to others your love, your generosity, your compassion, or that you care about them, there is some doubt in your own mind. For instance, you may have built up an image of what caring should look like in a particular relationship, and fear that yours doesn't measure up. No matter how hard you try to prove yourself, you will not get the results you want. What we feel the need to prove is almost never accepted by others; what we know to be true and make no special effort to express is instantly recognized.

Instead of focusing on how you *think* you should feel (loving, generous, understanding), try to see your true feelings clearly (respectful, appreciative, open). As you release old images and look at your connections with other people in a brighter light, the need to prove yourself will dissolve and true knowing will take its place.

Express the feelings you discover with compassion and appreciation for others. Concentrate on the positive feelings you have and the most satisfying aspects of being together. Others will respond to your compassionate and positive tone and find it easy to connect with you heart-to-heart. The truth of what you say will be unmistakable.

The compassion you need to carry your truth is flowing all around you —it is as available as the air you breathe. It exists in the deep caring you feel for those you love, the hope that every blessing will come to them. Acting with compassion does not mean that you should try to bring every blessing to their doorsteps yourself, but that if you had two wishes you would wish them joy and fulfillment, and sincerely mean it. Your compassion urges you to reach out in deeds or words to reinforce people's belief in themselves, to see their intrinsic value.

If you feel that you do not have access to a deep level of compassion, go back in your past and recall moments when you stopped and took from behind a dog's ear a burr that he was unable to dislodge with his paws, or when you held and comforted a crying baby or a friend in grief. Even if you once tried to shove those feelings aside as too soft or sentimental, you can recall them now by sitting quietly and asking the memories of compassion to surface. As compassion for yourself and others flows into your body, feel the tension drain away. Let the compassion envelop your mind. Feel yourself releasing the need to prove your love to anyone, including yourself.

1. Sit quietly and recall the deepest levels of compassion that you have experienced. Include childhood experiences with animals or pets, as well as with people.
2. Think about someone in your life to whom you have felt the need to prove something—your intelligence, your love, your generosity, your ability. Whatever it was, make a note of it.
3. See what was behind the need to prove. Notice that, no matter how hard you tried, you did not get the results you wanted.
4. In the flow of your compassionate knowing, see what your actual connection is to this person, free of all ideas about how to express it. Take her with you in your imagination to the top of a mountain and see the two of you standing there together with the sun shining warmly on your faces. Look into her eyes and resolve to express the truth of your wisdom. Feel the flow of compassion surrounding both of you.
5. You have created a pathway to your compassionate knowing. You are now ready to enjoy a deeper connection with this person in real life. Prepare to welcome new and revitalizing experiences together.

CHAPTER 48

Beyond Sympathy: Acting from Compassion

Sympathy and compassion may seem like the same emotion, but the difference between them is crucial. In sympathy you experience what other people are experiencing, in order to share their plight. If misery likes company, the sympathetic person is quick to provide it. If someone has a headache or a heartache, the sympathetic friend gets one too. Compassion comes from a different sphere. Rather than leap into the mud puddle that others have slipped into, you reach out from the curb and help them climb out and shake off their boots.

If you were about to drown you would hope for a person of compassion, not sympathy. Wouldn't you rather have a calm bystander throw you a life-preserver and pull you to shore than have a sympathetic person leap into the surging water and exhaust himself swimming out to you?

Instead of feeling sorry for someone close to you who is going through a difficult time—the path of sympathy—watch for and acknowledge that person's determination to meet the challenge. Point out his perseverance, not vaguely but in detail. Talk about the steps he is already taking to meet the challenge. Listen carefully and encourage him to describe how he will know when he has met the challenge. Watch his face glow as he visualizes himself there. He will feel your belief in him and it will strengthen his belief in himself.

If someone offers you sympathy, run fast in the other direction, for sympathy will tempt you to feel sorry for yourself. (Sympathy for yourself is self-pity. Compassion is understanding from the heart.) If you accept sympathy from those around you, they take the role of strength, leaving you the role of weakness. Remember that challenges and problems never imply weakness; rather, they are an opportunity for expansion in strength, love, and power.

If you are going through a difficult time, take a good look at what you *would* like to create out of the situation at hand—and ask your friends to envision that outcome for you. You don't need to tell them the details of your present difficulties, for some of your friends might become confused and focus on the difficulties rather than on the vision of what you want. When your friends envision you as successful and joyful, as flowing with creativity, you gain more strength and clarity to be that.

Resist all temptation to feel sorry for anyone. In order to feel sympathy you must hold a picture of the other person as being weaker than you— an image that person may accept as real, and thus need even more sympathy. Instead, offer compassion. Show that you genuinely care in every way you can. Remind her of her perseverance, encourage her to list practical steps to take, and then offer her help wherever you can.

Acting with compassion allows you to let go of needing to advise. It allows you to give freely without expecting anything back. Any time you shift from sympathy to true compassion, you will release an enormous reserve of gentleness, kindness, and grace with which you can truly help your loved ones to triumph.

1. Think of a few people with whom you have recently been tempted to sympathize.
2. What is the best situation you can imagine for each of them?
3. If the pictures in your mind are like snapshots, let them come to life as movies. Watch these people live out their movies, enjoying their new-found success.

Part VII

TRUSTING YOUR TRUE SELF

CHAPTER 49

Beyond Making a Good Impression: Radiating Inner Beauty

Whenever we feel a need to make a good impression, we are trying to live up to what we believe are other people's standards. We press upon ourselves an image that is not our own. Having to live up to such an image is a barrier to real connections. It not only inhibits connecting with others, but also prevents us from connecting with our own inner beauty.

When we try to figure out how to be someone others will like, we become self-conscious and usually decide our ordinary, real self is not good enough. Very skilled people can persuade others that they are other than who they really are, but even they can carry it off for only a very brief time. When we try to be actors, we miss the chance to truly connect.

Often our anxieties are related to self-doubts about our bodies, and especially our faces. Remember that your face and body serve as vehicles for true expression of your self. Every time you look in the mirror and feel critical of any aspect of your appearance, you are distancing yourself from your own inner beauty and draining your energy. In contrast, when you acknowledge and honor your inner beauty, you will feel a new surge of power. Your body will be enlivened by this new energy flowing freely through you; your sparkling eyes and smile will then express who you truly are.

The same is true of your mind. As you develop more awareness of the wisdom of your true self, you will no longer feel unsure about what to say when you meet new people, nor will you be concerned about the impression you are making on someone who seems more knowledgeable than you.

Think of someone you especially admire for the quality of his or her mind. The very fact that you recognize that quality demonstrates that some aspect of it is also within you. It would be difficult to recognize it if it were not part of your experience, just as it is impossible to appreciate a great violinist's genius unless you have had some experience with music.

Whenever you are grateful to be who you are, beyond the judgments you or anyone else may make, you radiate inner beauty. Any time you are doing something you love, whether it is sailing, cleaning out the garage, or having lunch with a good friend, your delight in what you are doing allows your inner beauty to radiate for all to see. When a woman throws back her head and laughs with genuine humor, you will admire her beauty regardless of her age or facial features. Yet that beauty would disappear quickly if she were only pretending to be light and humorous in order to make a good impression on someone she believed to be important.

Instead of worrying about making an impression when you are introduced to new people—even if they are powerful or important—speak to them with genuine interest, anticipating a pleasing communication. Only when you lose touch with your innate beauty and forget who you really are do you stop your inner flow of vitality. All of us have that energy; we have only to remember it.

1. Take a few minutes to become aware of the life spirit that animates you. Sitting erect and comfortable, with your eyes closed, breathe deeply. Feel the energy in your feet for a few minutes. Then move your attention to your calves and up to your thighs. Move upward slowly to your hips, stomach, chest, heart, shoulders, and arms, hands, and fingers. Then feel the same energy coursing through your spinal column and neck, your head and face. You can increase the flow of this energy by briefly focusing on it in any part of your body.

2. Choose where you wish your inner radiance to express itself first in your physical body—your eyes, your smile, your hands. Then spend a couple of minutes focusing on that part until you feel a tingling or pulsing there.

3. Your mind and emotions respond in the same way. If you want the quality of joy, for example, focus on what it means to you and the feeling it brings. Once your mind is directed toward joy and immersed in it, joy will follow.

4. Now think of a situation (intimate or social) in which you might be anxious about making a good impression and take that just-created feeling of joy into the situation. See yourself enter the room with a radiant, joyful feeling. Hear yourself speak and respond to others; notice how gracefully you accept their appreciation of you—spoken and unspoken—just as you are.

CHAPTER 50

Beyond Confusion: Trusting Your Intuition

We feel confusion when we stand between letting go of an old way of seeing and choosing a new way. No one enjoys feeling confused, yet it is a sign that we are expanding the framework of our lives. When we make major decisions, such as moving to a new community, marrying, or divorcing, we nearly always go through a period of confusion before we see clearly again. While we are confused, we may think we have lost our path and try to go back to where we were before. It never works. All we can do is move forward, feeling our way, trying out each possibility in our minds before we jump into it.

Sometimes many voices, representing different dimensions of ourselves, compete to influence our decisions. The voice from our past echoes the way we have always thought about a person or situation. It suggests the familiar thing to do. The invaluable voice of intuition comes soft and subtle, like a light breeze on our faces. We feel it, but don't know immediately where it came from. It keeps coming back with the same message, sometimes for a year or more, until we pay attention. Rather than using language, it reaches us with images, sometimes flashing a picture of the likely outcome of an action. It's as if our inner self shows us the end of several movies so that we can select the one we want to be in.

You may sense the presence of your intuition when you are on the threshold of sleep, either going into it or coming out of it. The times when you are still and quiet, not doing anything at all, are the easiest to open to your intuitive knowing. We all have had moments of doing this. We have all acted without a logical reason, without trying to explain or justify our action.

To recall your moments of intuition, you have only to remember a time when you came out of a fog and suddenly saw with new understanding and clarity. Sometimes quietly, sometimes in a flash, when you were neither looking back nor worrying about what's ahead, intuition has come through to point you in the best direction.

When it happens, you see clearly. You suddenly know how to create harmony in the family, how to handle your daughter's rebellion, how to heal a friend in grief. The answer seems so obvious that you realize that you have always known it. Your intuition is always there, waiting patiently for a listening ear.

1. When you hear the voice of intuition, consider whether the idea it suggests is similar to ideas or images that have come to you, no matter how briefly, over the months or years. If so, they will probably continue to visit you until you respond in some way.
2. Consider whether the action you are considering would harm anyone else. Your intuition would not harm others; neither would it be subjected to someone else's authority.
3. If you're considering alternatives, consider whether you feel a surge of energy as you think of a particular choice of action. True intuition is energizing.
4. Sit quietly alone and focus on the situation that confuses you. If any distracting thoughts come to you, imagine that you are putting them in an envelope and mailing them away. Examine the choices of action that occur to you. Acknowledge the seed of truth in each one. The greater your sense of appreciation, the more open you are to your true intuition.

CHAPTER 51

Beyond Loneliness: Discovering the Self as Companion

Being alone is not the same as being lonely. When we want time alone and get it, we enjoy ourselves. But when we interpret solitude as being forsaken by friends, we feel lonely and miserable, especially if we decide we are "left out" or "don't belong."

We may even feel lonely when we *are* with other people. Our loneliness at such times is not for outside companionship, but for an inner connection.

Most of us alternate between embracing and resisting being alone. When we resist time alone, we fill every hour with work, entertainment, projects. Unfortunately, by staying busy, we miss the experience of simply being with our silent or true selves. Only when we are not responding to another person or project do we have the opportunity to be with this self. So long as we are busy with people, it remains dormant and unrecognized.

When we embrace our time alone, we become adventurers. We become intrigued with a part of ourselves that has been in hiding. A most enticing companion, this self is close to our source of life and always responds when summoned. Our true self does not reprimand, preach, badger, accuse, or demand. It does counsel, caution, warn, suggest, recommend, and invite. The minute you make a connection with this companion you know that all loneliness is an illusion.

Since the self does not originate in the brain, you can miss being aware of its presence. But you can connect with your true self when you sit quietly and wait for it to appear. As you sit, quiet and yet alert, you will feel peaceful. You may want to focus on a specific ideal—such as love or wisdom—until you notice ideas popping up, seemingly from nowhere, about yourself or specific situations. Or you can focus on strength and become aware of a powerful feeling of being centered. If you focus on clarity, you will notice an altered and refreshing understanding.

If you have questions, ask them. Ask if accepting this job is your wisest decision, or moving to a new city is a good idea. After that, ask how to expand your love for your daughter, your friend, or your lover. Assume that the answer is being silently relayed to your brain and that when you need it, the ideas and impulse for new action will be there. Many people hear or feel the response in their minds, or in bodies. The "yes" response is easiest to observe. It often comes as a tingling in your hands or fingers or in your head.

Don't expect to be chastised, punished, criticized, or judged by your silent self. If that should happen, you are witnessing a rebellion by the part of you that wants to judge, the part that wants to achieve, or the part that feels threatened by loss of control. Your silent self does not function that way. Rather, watch for suggestions of alternative ways of looking at situations—more gentle, forgiving, loving ways that bring you peace. Expect to feel calm about your life, to understand your friends better and appreciate them far more than you do now.

Be aware that you will reach a cut-off point. All of us soon hit our limit for accepting communication of this caliber. We then find a certain comfort in what is familiar, even if that means loneliness. When you hit your limit you may go to sleep or suddenly jump up, remembering an errand. You may "forget" for a while to set time alone, and continue to fill your days and evenings with people—both in person and on the television screen. But each time you go back to your true self, you can receive a little more from the infinite well of wisdom and truth that is waiting for you.

At the end of each session with your silent self, acknowledge what you have gained—*even if you think you are making it all up.* Take notes and date them. This way you can check out the degree of wisdom that has come forth as the weeks pass.

By the authority of your own inner will, you can create time alone as soon as you wish. Who does not deserve the compassion and the wisdom that only his or her true self can offer? The closer you become to your silent self, the more fulfilling your time with others will be. For the only thing of true value that we have to pass on to the people around us is the knowledge and love that *we* receive in our sessions with our true selves.

1. Make time to be alone, free from interruption. Sit in a comfortable position with your back supported and straight. Play soft music if you need to block out other voices or noise. Think about the abundance of time, the willingness to be surprised, the peacefulness that is about to come over you.

2. Begin to observe where each breath goes. Experiment with breathing deeply and easily. Imagine the vitality of the air reaching and refreshing each part of your body. Imagine each breath bringing you

clarity and serenity until you begin to feel a satisfying sense of stillness within.

3. Rather than focus on a problem you don't want (such as struggle and effort), focus on a solution you do want. When you finish, write the positive action you now see is possible, no matter where you think the ideas came from.

CHAPTER 52

Beyond Rejection: Reconnecting with Your True Self

We all know many people. Some we consider to be friends; a few we confide in as intimates. As we meet new people, we choose the ones who will fit into our busy lives. So long as we respond honestly and openly to each person we meet, we can share the warmth of our mutual humanity regardless of the number of minutes we spend together.

A six-year-old girl in the grocery store with her mother suddenly announced that she was going to dance for a new friend. She skipped from the brussel sprouts to the endive, whirled in front of the cherry tomatoes, and with three great leaps circled the African violets. Then she folded her body into a sweeping bow.

A small boy—her audience—stood spellbound while the girl's mother and other shoppers busily fingered the peaches and pineapples. The two children had met at the strawberries only minutes before. Chances are they will never see each other again, but for a few moments they shared a real connection. The opportunities to connect are everywhere. An opportunity passed up is not rejection. We reject others only when we are not willing to acknowledge the true value they have within. How is it, then, that rejection comes up so often as we meet new people?

Have you ever had an immediate negative reaction to a person you hardly know? Or have you ever found yourself disturbed by personality traits in another person that others simply overlook? Occasionally, we meet someone who reminds us of a trait within us that we have rejected. We quickly turn away, from the trait and from the person. We confuse the trait (shyness, trying too hard, trying to impress) with "who we are," and immediately look for a reason to dismiss the person who unknowingly makes us uncomfortable. "He must want something," or "has nothing to offer me," is "uninteresting," or "insensitive." Any reason will do. And a potential friend is lost.

Sometimes we fear rejection from a person to whom we want to reach out. We associate memories of feeling rejected by others with the person standing in front of us, often with astonishingly little reason. "This man is tall. My husband is tall, and he left me for another woman." Or, "This woman talks softly; I can't trust her. My girlfriend talked softly—and married another man." Once we've attached an old hurt to the new person, the connection is doomed. At the first silence after "hello," we turn tail and run—like a skittish deer, before overtures of friendship can be made or accepted.

Sometimes we miss a connection because we misjudge a new person. A person who stumbles over words, even one who remains nearly silent, may actually be more open to receiving our friendship than someone who seems more friendly. Shy people often respond automatically with polite words that hide their real feelings, even when the person inside longs to connect.

Rather than worrying about whether you will be accepted or rejected, try going toward people and openly accepting everyone you can. Enjoy a variety of friends and interest groups. People who share your delight in singing, art, sculpting, music, bird-watching, or hiking will enhance your appreciation of yourself and may soon become friends as well. If you depend on only one person for a sense of acceptance and well-being, and that person rejects your artistic or recreational interests, you could feel rejected as a person. With a circle of supportive friends, you will find it easier to keep a wise perspective on the total being that you are.

You, like all people, have a gemstone, a true self, hidden deep inside you. Trust it. Only by trusting in the inherent pricelessness of our own true selves can we accept and appreciate others. Since the true self does not have a visible form and can only wait patiently for our attention, our more assertive sides easily divert our time and energy away from it. You can reconnect with your separated self by taking charge of a tiny portion of your day and using it to uncover more of who you are.

When you identify (even momentarily) with the self that beckons you to meaning and purpose, you will have more compassion for the less-developed sides of yourself. Our personalities lag far behind our true selves in wisdom and compassion. That is why a sense of peace follows a moment of higher identification. The more you recognize your true self, the stronger and more frequent a part of your life that state of peace will become. Whenever you are in it, you will naturally accept others—even if you meet only briefly.

1. When someone seems to reject you, ask yourself what were your hopes, fears, and expectations about relating to that person. Distinguish between rejection of your beliefs and rejection of you.

2. Remember being honored as a valuable person by a friend, a parent, or a child. Imagine ways you can express your true self more fully with several important people in your life.

3. Establish a relationship between your ordinary state of awareness and your true self. Imagine being in a pool of gentle light, or joining with an image of light—any form of prayer or meditation that helps you to make this connection.

Part VIII

"TAKE ACTION" CARDS

1

Beyond present boundaries

Opening new territory

2

Beyond practicality

Daring to invent

3

Beyond expectation

Accepting surprises

4

Beyond self-discipline

Savoring spontaneous moments

5

Beyond fixed positions

Increasing flexibility

6

Beyond forgiveness

Reinterpreting and releasing the past

7

Beyond compromise

Expanding the range of choices

8

Beyond present possibilities

Exploring a larger you

CONNECTING
With All the People
in Your Life

CONNECTING
With All the People
in Your Life

CONNECTING
With All the People
in Your Life

CONNECTING
With All the People
in Your Life

CONNECTING
With All the People
in Your Life

CONNECTING
With All the People
in Your Life

CONNECTING
With All the People
in Your Life

CONNECTING
With All the People
in Your Life

9

Beyond withdrawing

Finding your true center

10

Beyond pride

Clarifying your desires

11

Beyond holding on

Beginning again

12

Beyond irritation

Appreciating separate realities

13

Beyond blame

Embracing underlying intentions

14

Beyond guilt

Releasing phantoms

15

Beyond dependency

Experiencing inner strength

16

Beyond reacting

Choosing the waves to ride

CONNECTING
With All the People
in Your Life

CONNECTING
With All the People
in Your Life

CONNECTING
With All the People
in Your Life

CONNECTING
With All the People
in Your Life

CONNECTING
With All the People
in Your Life

CONNECTING
With All the People
in Your Life

CONNECTING
With All the People
in Your Life

CONNECTING
With All the People
in Your Life

17

Beyond spending time together

Choosing to connect

18

Beyond fate

Weaving a new future

19

Beyond ambivalence

Acting on deeper commitments

20

Beyond hope and fear

Taking action, however small

21

Beyond restlessness

Carrying out the intention to connect

22

Beyond assertiveness

Acting from genuine power

23

Beyond deserving

Moving with trust and intention

24

Beyond struggle and effort

Allowing playfulness

CONNECTING
With All the People
in Your Life

CONNECTING
With All the People
in Your Life

CONNECTING
With All the People
in Your Life

CONNECTING
With All the People
in Your Life

CONNECTING
With All the People
in Your Life

CONNECTING
With All the People
in Your Life

CONNECTING
With All the People
in Your Life

CONNECTING
With All the People
in Your Life

25

Beyond feeling shy or hesitant

Enjoying self-expression

26

Beyond delaying or avoiding

Expressing honest responses

27

Beyond persuasion

Offering and inviting

28

Beyond "hearing"

Listening with alert compassion

29

Beyond swallowing back feelings

Expressing yourself clearly

30

Beyond being articulate

Speaking from innate wisdom

31

Beyond embarrassment

Speaking out with honesty

32

Beyond words

Communicating in silence

CONNECTING
With All the People
in Your Life

CONNECTING
With All the People
in Your Life

CONNECTING
With All the People
in Your Life

CONNECTING
With All the People
in Your Life

CONNECTING
With All the People
in Your Life

CONNECTING
With All the People
in Your Life

CONNECTING
With All the People
in Your Life

CONNECTING
With All the People
in Your Life

33

Beyond fear and caution

Opening to adventure

34

Beyond possessiveness

Assuring mutual freedom

35

Beyond hero worship

Appreciating your inherent qualities

36

Beyond seriousness

Experiencing lightness and humor

37

Beyond obligation

Living from free choice

38

Beyond jealousy

Releasing with a blessing

39

Beyond need

Accepting innate abundance

40

Beyond control

Affirming autonomy

CONNECTING
With All the People
in Your Life

CONNECTING
With All the People
in Your Life

CONNECTING
With All the People
in Your Life

CONNECTING
With All the People
in Your Life

CONNECTING
With All the People
in Your Life

CONNECTING
With All the People
in Your Life

CONNECTING
With All the People
in Your Life

CONNECTING
With All the People
in Your Life

41

Beyond right and wrong

Recognizing the wisdom of the heart

42

Beyond being reasonable

Knowing the ways of the heart

43

Beyond having things in common

Sharing the ability to envision

44

Beyond pressure to do

Embracing your stillness

45

Beyond established roles

Engaging from the heart

46

Beyond relief

Experiencing delight

47

Beyond proving

Knowing from within

48

Beyond sympathy

Acting from compassion

CONNECTING
With All the People
in Your Life

CONNECTING
With All the People
in Your Life

CONNECTING
With All the People
in Your Life

CONNECTING
With All the People
in Your Life

CONNECTING
With All the People
in Your Life

CONNECTING
With All the People
in Your Life

CONNECTING
With All the People
in Your Life

CONNECTING
With All the People
in Your Life

49

Beyond making a good impression

Radiating inner beauty

50

Beyond confusion

Trusting your intuition

51

Beyond loneliness

Discovering the self as companion

52

Beyond rejection

Reconnecting with your true self

53

Beyond acquiescence

Respecting the authority of your true self

54

Beyond security

Discovering inner resources

55

Beyond internal conflict

Honoring integrity

56

Beyond "going somewhere"

Appreciating where you are now

CONNECTING
With All the People
in Your Life

CONNECTING
With All the People
in Your Life

CONNECTING
With All the People
in Your Life

CONNECTING
With All the People
in Your Life

CONNECTING
With All the People
in Your Life

CONNECTING
With All the People
in Your Life

CONNECTING
With All the People
in Your Life

CONNECTING
With All the People
in Your Life

57

Beyond superiority and inferiority

Recognizing basic nobility

58

Beyond agreement

Appreciating different beliefs

59

Beyond tact

Acknowledging strengths

60

Beyond attachment

Seeing the essence behind the form

61

Beyond helping

Empowering others

62

Beyond anger

Honoring the deeper common purpose

63

Beyond competition

Cooperating out of strength

64

Beyond giving or receiving

Sharing a joyful balance

CONNECTING
With All the People
in Your Life

CONNECTING
With All the People
in Your Life

CONNECTING
With All the People
in Your Life

CONNECTING
With All the People
in Your Life

CONNECTING
With All the People
in Your Life

CONNECTING
With All the People
in Your Life

CONNECTING
With All the People
in Your Life

CONNECTING
With All the People
in Your Life

CHAPTER 53

Beyond Acquiescence: Respecting the Authority of Your True Self

In the martial art called Aikido, acquiescence is an asset. Centering your body and your mind, you let your opponent come toward you, offering no resistance, saving your energy. If he pushes or lunges, you catch him off balance and gently, firmly, assist him to go past you, thus rendering him harmless. You are able to do this because you know where your center point is, and you are in it.

When you feel that you're giving in to someone else, go back to your center point. That is where you expand your capacity to love, gain understanding, transform your knowing into wisdom. Whatever the decision you are trying to make, see if compliance serves it. As long as you hold a clear vision in your mind, you will know when to let go of small preferences and when to stand up courageously in respect for your true identity.

If a difference of opinion arises with a friend or within a group, and the outcome affects neither you individually nor your purpose together, you are wise to express your amiable side, to let someone else take control, to go along with the group. If, on the other hand, a plan interferes with the authority of your own true self, you don't have to go along. Just use mental Aikido. Stand your ground and calmly allow the other's assumed authority to pass by you.

Take a brief look over past major relationships—ones in which you were genuinely involved. Focus on what you learned about when to acquiesce and when to honor your inner knowing. Daily struggles about who was in control, who was to lead, and who to follow were meaningless static. What difference did it make if the scenic route was winding and you got lost, the porridge was served too hot or too cold, or even who cooked it?

To distinguish the difference between automatic acquiescence and respecting your inner authority (choosing to acquiesce or not), look for your feeling of contraction or expansion in each relationship. Contraction is a "less than" feeling—less feelings of love, of abundance, of giving and receiving. It comes from automatic acquiescence. You stand straighter and breathe more deeply when you draw on your own authority. You feel expanded. When you use acquiescence appropriately, as a part of following your inner authority, you can gain a powerful balance in each relationship.

Balance is gained through experience, just as in learning to ride a bicycle. Reading about bicycle balance evokes your curiosity, even inspires you; seeing someone who rides well convinces you it's possible; but only getting on the bicycle—pedaling, guiding, leaning first to the left and then to the right—will teach the balance of freedom and delight.

1. Review your life as far back as you can remember. Think of times when you made important and wise choices, overlooking the presumed authority of others.

2. With eyes closed, see yourself becoming more amiable about daily details that don't really matter. Think of small conflicts at home and at work and imagine new responses.

3. Relax even more, lean against the back of your chair, and imagine a point of light about 6 inches above your head. Focus on this point and imagine you are tuning in to the vibration of your true self, receiving and integrating its silent messages.

4. Think of yourself as having a wise and loving guide who communicates to you through your intuition, not just in crises, but in making everyday choices that will bring harmony and delight into each connection you have.

CHAPTER 54

Beyond Security: Discovering Inner Resources

Our need for security rises and falls according to our ability to tune in to our own inner resources. Money and power are our primary outside sources of security. For a brief while, they give us an illusory sense of safety. But soon we start needing more. What once seemed like enough no longer gives us a secure feeling. No matter how much money or power we get, we can't stop our insecurities from surfacing again without warning.

The same is true when we seek security through someone else's love. We become so dependent on that love that we are soon prisoners in our own house of illusion, blind to the fact that nothing outside of ourselves can feed our need for real security. Constantly seeking assurances from our partner, we squeeze more and more of our life energy into one limited area of the relationship. We sacrifice joy in order to feel security.

Imagine trying the opposite approach. Decide to experiment with a particular relationship in your life, giving up any concern for security. Instead of trying to guarantee that the other person will be there for you tomorrow, simply be totally present with him or her now, at this moment. No matter whom you're with, act as if you have nothing to lose. Like the cat that jumps out of a tree and always lands on its feet, you too will land on your feet—so long as you are in a state of good humor and express yourself honestly. You have an endless source of new ideas inside you. Let them start bubbling up to enhance your relationship. Express what you feel; suggest new things to do together. Respecting your own feelings in this way dramatically changes how you feel about yourself; respecting your friends' feelings will change how you feel about them.

You will quickly discover new levels of confidence, understanding, courage, and truth that you never suspected were in you. At the end of a week, look back and notice the difference in the vitality of your friendship. As you let go of thoughts of outer security, you will realize that seeking a sense of security through someone else's love or support is not only illusory but exhausting—it takes a great deal of energy to hide from the realization of the enormous love and compassion within you.

You'll enjoy and appreciate other people's support and caring even more when you know you don't need them to make you feel whole. Once you let go of the illusion of security in a relationship, you will find that your own strength and love provide abundantly for you.

1. Make a list of things that would make you feel secure in a specific relationship (e.g., caring, companionship).
2. Now imagine that your partner has fulfilled everything on the list. Precisely how would your life be different? If your partner thought of these things as obligations, rather than as spontaneous desires from the heart, would you still feel secure?
3. List your own inner resources (everything you have that can't be taxed, stolen, or burned). Everyone has many resources that have been misfiled in someone else's life file. Take a dozen manila folders and label each with a resource that *will* give you security: "courage," "confidence," "creativity," "opening to adventure," "truthfulness," "sense of humor," and so forth. File them under "Personal Inner Resources." During the next few weeks, jot down every situation in which you express one of these qualities and file it in the appropriate folder. No situation can be too minor to be filed; the resource is the same regardless of the magnitude of the event. If you spend a few minutes each evening, you will soon have a fascinating collection. The point is to take a close look at your vast storehouse of resources. (If you prefer, you can do this exercise in your mind instead of on paper.)
4. After a few weeks of developing and strengthening your inner security, cross off the items on your list from step 1, as appropriate.

CHAPTER 55

Beyond Internal Conflict: Honoring Integrity

We have all dreamed of having three wishes, the third being a wish for everything we didn't wish for in the first two. There are so many things we think we want, three wishes never seem like enough. And past experience teaches us that what we will want six months from now may be altogether different from what we want today. When we feel pulled in many directions at once by conflicting desires and changing perspectives, we find it hard to make lasting connections that offer true satisfaction. How can we give our solemn word about anything and then stand solidly behind that commitment a year later—sometimes a month later?

Many of the conflicts that get in the way of fulfilling connections with our friends and family are conflicts not with them, but within ourselves. Each side of ourselves has its own goal. One may want higher education, another more money, a third an ideal marriage, and a fourth some rank and status. We can't commit our full energy to any one goal, because a different part of us takes control each day.

Each side of yourself is like a child that has to be educated to recognize and to honor *your* highest values. It would be foolish to grant autocratic rule to any one of them; nor do you want a democracy in which each side of yourself has an equal vote. One would vote for reading all day, one for working diligently to get ahead, one for making love—what kind of result would you get?

When your various sides disagree and struggle to get the upper hand, you feel your inner clarity and sense of purpose fade. The bright light of who you are is blocked. These sides tend to make a big deal of things that don't really matter in the long run. Learn to recognize their ploys and treat them with compassion, as you would a pouting child who wants to control the other children.

To bring your true self out from behind the clouds, look for the major goals of each side of yourself. Note each one as you find it. Soon you will have a picture of your internal conflict. Learn everything you can about these goals by imagining a conversation with each side of yourself. Picture yourself introducing your various sides to each other—especially the opposing ones. Gradually, you will establish more harmony between them. As the director of the saga of your life, tell them the plot and rehearse them on their parts. Each has skills that can serve you well.

As you gain their cooperation you will increase your ability to speak and act, and to commit to a project, a relationship, a life career with integrity —with your whole self behind it—without sabotage.

When you act from your highest purpose, what you say or do will be more likely to come from your own integrity. It happens with one choice, one word, one act at a time. There is no sudden dramatic moment when all the parts of your personality snap to attention.

As the clouds of conflict disperse, you will feel in touch with your true self, and others will sense this. There is a different expression on the faces of people who are clearly focused on a single purpose.

Communicating with integrity—from the united stand of all the sides of yourself—may sound like an impossible ideal. But all it means is that you have integrated the needs of your different sides, and that you trust in your true self to direct the show. Once you see the power of this trust, you will know why integrity offers the most reasonable and wise approach to relationships.

With your own life under the direction of your integrity it will be easier to recognize that same integrity in others and honor it as you do your own. Two or more people working with the single-minded commitment that only integrity offers can work in a powerful rhythm of harmony that affects not only their own lives, but the life of their community and everyone they come into contact with.

1. Select three major sides of yourself, each with different and conflicting goals, and imagine having a conversation with them about the drama of your life.
2. Find out what they want from you and tell them what you want from them.
3. Choose one relationship in which you feel you have conflicting goals. What is the one major value you want to achieve from that relationship? Talk to each of your sides about that goal and show them how to use their specific skills to reach it.

CHAPTER 56

Beyond "Going Somewhere": Appreciating Where You Are Now

Can you imagine a hungry bear scooping a fish from the brook, only to throw it down and go after a bigger one? Bears don't do that. They eat with relish the fish they catch and then move on to catch another one.

Sometimes, in the people kingdom, we step over the opportunity in front of us to pursue another version of the same opportunity. Unlike the bear, we cast aside what's already in our hands without ever seeing its value. We are so intent on new and more exciting experiences that we miss the beauty in what we have now.

Perhaps, without realizing it, fixed or automatic routines have come between you and the people who mean the most to you—separating you from the best connection possible. When this happens, a relationship can't move into greater depths of compassionate giving and receiving, of speaking out with honesty, or of honoring the true self in each of you. It is easy to decide in frustration that that relationship isn't going anywhere.

None of us can go anywhere until we truly appreciate the relationship that is possible now. It is up to us to find ideas to enrich our present situation by asking, "What *would* happen if I were more loving, forgiving, thoughtful, even playful?" We have nothing to lose and everything to gain by seeing for ourselves what would happen if we were outrageously compassionate and understanding for just one week.

Dare to try out every idea that *might* make a difference in your present situation. Otherwise, any change is premature. You would always look back and wonder if you *could* have transformed a tentative or conditional love into a wholehearted one by acting on the ideas you had.

If we don't put our full effort into the present situation, we are likely to find the same challenges in our next relationship. (If you don't feel equal, appreciated, and loved in your current relationship, and move into another one *prematurely,* you may find yourself not feeling equal, appreciated, and loved in the second one.)

Imagine you are the bear and one of your relationships is the fish in your paw. Rather than throw it back, take a second look to see exactly what kind of fish is in your hand. You may have thought it was a mackerel, but you now discover that it's an Alaskan salmon. Taste your fish again, this time expecting it to taste like what it really is, and see if you don't enjoy it more.

Even if you had the best salmon in the world, it would taste pretty flat if you thought it was a mackerel. If you have a present relationship that is less than fully satisfying, look for the specific trait or quality that you are learning from it—perhaps compassion, understanding, a greater ability to enjoy yourself, even to laugh at yourself.

When you identify this quality, look back to past relationships in which it was also challenged. See how far you have come since then. Now imagine this trait as a powerful and refined asset in your future. Imagine how you will be more open, inventive, and aware of your innate abundance.

Your acknowledgment of the past and the future allows you to relax and enjoy what is happening now—to relish the fish that you have in your hands, to forget about the future until you have fully lived the present. There is a story about a monk who lived for the future. This devout monk wanted only to be enlightened so he would be free from the endless round of lifetimes on earth. Finally, he was granted a brief hearing with the great master in a faraway village. He approached the master in deep reverence and respectfully said:

"Master, I have sacrificed every pleasure in life. I have fasted, given alms to the poor, prayed faithfully six times a day. Please tell me, how many lifetimes do I have left?"

The master was silent for a long time and then told the monk that he still had three more lifetimes. The monk moaned in despair and said, "Oh, woe is me, three more lifetimes to sacrifice, to endure the miseries of this earth, to live in isolation."

And he turned away in deep sorrow and disappointment.

The town juggler was standing nearby and, not knowing that he did not "deserve" a hearing with this great master, shyly walked up to him and spoke:

"Sir, I don't know anything about religion. I have never fasted. I don't even know how to pray well. Can you tell me how many lifetimes I have left?"

The master nodded, smiled, and said in a compassionate tone, "Son, you have a thousand more lifetimes."

"Oh, Joy! Joy! Joy!" the juggler exclaimed. "A thousand more lifetimes to play with the children, to teach them, to make them laugh, and to sing."

And in that instant he was enlightened—and freed from any more lifetimes on earth.

Think of yourself as the juggler. Act as if you feel the way he did about your life and relationships, just as they are now. As soon as you exalt in the joy of the present moment, it will change to a new experience. Each person you laugh and sing with, teach or learn from, can give you a new awareness of who you really are. Let every awakening to your beauty and the beauty of others around you be cause for celebration.

1. Think of the relationships that you have now. What is the most wondrous thing about each? If you can't decide on one outstanding thing, name two.
2. Write a note to each of these people. Express simply and directly what you find wondrous in knowing them.
3. If you desire to feel some of the delight of the juggler, how can you reach out to know and enjoy more people in your life? Include people you do not know—children, foreign residents, new people in your town, students, retired people.

Part IX

HONORING THE TRUE SELF OF OTHERS

CHAPTER 57

Beyond Superiority and Inferiority: Recognizing Basic Nobility

A lion is inferior to an elephant in its ability to carry heavy loads, yet superior in its speed and ability to hunt. Both have a basic nobility. Any time we compare ourselves to someone else, we have no choice but to feel either inferior or superior. The outcome depends on whom we compare ourselves to. After we compare ourselves to a person who makes us feel inferior, we feel bad, so we look for someone who makes us feel superior. It's a never-ending seesaw.

All of us can make ourselves feel inferior to almost any peer in *some* area of our lives. And, equally as easily, we can make ourselves feel superior. Imagine sitting at a dinner party where the person on your left stimulates in you an inferior feeling, and the person on your right a superior one. Each time you look to the left, you feel inferior and each time you look to the right, superior. Switch your attention back and forth between these dinner partners and you'll soon get dizzy, as opposite images of yourself collide.

The secret of balance lies not in alternating between feelings of inferiority and superiority, but in finding a true sense of who you are. Your true self is aware of the inner nobility that exists not only within you, but within everyone. Any moment you truly recognize this nobility in yourself, you are also able to see it in the people you are with. For example, you see someone in need and go out of your way to assist simply because you want to do so. In the natural exhilaration that follows, you feel a spark of your own nobility. That positive feeling changes the way you look at the world, and for days afterward you find it easy to sense the same spark within everyone you meet.

As you learn to recognize the nobility in yourself and in others, you begin to enjoy the rich variety of roles that each of us is playing in the world. You will probably experience three changes: new enthusiasm for meeting people and renewing old friendships, greater awareness of nobility in the people closest to you, and an ability to connect with people in less time than ever before. (Notice how direct your speech becomes, and how you look people straight in the eye when you talk to them— including people in power.)

Let this way of perceiving yourself and others become a habit that gently pulses in your thoughts, and in every cell of your body. As you experience this view of yourself and of others, the urge to be superior and the fear of feeling inferior will soon disappear.

People intuitively know our underlying judgment of ourselves and of them. Every time we release the need to judge, we widen the range of people we enjoy—new opportunities arise from unexpected sources. And when we recognize and appreciate the nobility within all of us, we make new and deeper friendships.

1. Your own heartbeat can help you gain an awareness of basic nobility. Imagine that your heart is beating in rhythm with the heart of another—someone to whom you feel inferior or superior. In your imagination, acknowledge to that person that you share an inner nobility.
2. If there is someone in your life who intimidates you, imagine yourself sitting with that person on a deserted island. Quietly talk together about who you are *beneath* the obvious differences.
3. Spend time with the people who give you a good feeling about yourself. Decide what you want to learn from them and how you will know you are learning it.
4. Silently acknowledge several times today (and all week) that you— *and* each person you see—have an inner nobility.

Beyond Agreement: Honoring Different Beliefs

Think of the way you feel when a friend nods enthusiastically and says, "Yes, I agree," after you have shared a heartfelt belief. Agreement is music to everyone's ears.

Disagreement is disturbing to everyone. If we feel we know what we are talking about and someone disagrees, we naturally want to straighten her out as soon as possible. In our zeal we may even begin to express stronger and stronger opinions. Or, in place of trying to persuade others, we may be tempted to do the opposite—to withdraw in silence, smiling with sealed lips or staring intently at the ceiling.

Another way we avoid disagreement is simply by not "hearing" it. Or we may fantasize that the other person really means something different from what he said. Sometimes we totally avoid subjects on which we expect disagreement. The price of that tactic is high. Sooner or later we have to carry around a long mental list to remember who disagrees with what.

Among our convictions we all have some about which we feel strongly —yet we are not challenged when people disagree with them. These are beliefs born of personal experience. For instance, if your friend disagrees with your taste for vacations in Alaska rather than on warm tropical islands, you are not upset. You don't feel the need to change his mind. Instead, you would probably find his experiences fascinating and share yours with ease.

Our problems arise in areas where we lack direct experience and have simply borrowed ideas from someone else—a parent, a spouse, an author. We are easily thrown off balance when someone questions those ideas, no matter how wise they originally sounded to us. When our beliefs are inherited rather than original, even small differences of opinion can mushroom into arguments. Two friends spent three wonderful weeks together on a Hawaiian island. One day at lunch one of them wanted to order cantaloupe, but the other insisted it is not healthy to eat melon with a meal. They argued passionately, until one of them realized they were both quoting what others had told them. Neither was really looking at the truth about melons from her own experience.

Take a closer look when you find yourself wanting others to agree with you. Does your point of view come from someone else or your own experience? Once you clarify your own beliefs, you will be more open to enjoying the different beliefs of others.

Be glad for all areas of disagreement. They give you an opportunity to expand your world of interest by understanding the views of others. Rather than judge another person as dull or short-sighted because her beliefs do not validate and support yours, ask with genuine interest how she reached her conclusions. As she tells you, you can share her experience through her description.

When you ask a person what he *believes* to be true, his response usually arises out of a cluster of doubts. Ask him what he *knows for sure* to be true, and he will respond with his beliefs. Listen carefully. You will become intrigued, and you may discover surprising areas of agreement beyond surface differences.

Challenge yourself to learn more about the belief behind the one he is talking about. As you question him in an open and appreciative way, you will be able to see many of your own views in a new light. When you find a person who enjoys being invited to look beyond each belief, follow your mutual interests. You will eventually reach the fundamental ideas on which a great part of his life is based. At that moment you will both feel a very close connection, and a deep sense of common experience.

1. Choose one subject on which you would regard a differing point of view as an opportunity to venture into someone else's world. Imagine listening to the other person's point of view with alert interest.
2. Imagine asking more questions, learning more, and getting a sense of the validity of the other viewpoint.
3. Recall an occasion when somebody else's way of looking at one of your favorite subjects gave you enjoyment. Every time you discover such an occasion, notice how solid you feel about yourself in this area. Look for new areas of your life in which you can honor someone else's beliefs.

CHAPTER 59

Beyond Tact: Acknowledging Strengths

Tact is an essential skill. It smooths relationships and softens uncomfortable situations. We all use tact out of respect for people's feelings and self-esteem. We are also tactful when *we* feel uncomfortable in a situation —when we turn down certain invitations, show dissatisfaction with someone's work, express unpleasant reactions.

Sometimes, however, we misuse this tool. We use tact to circle around an issue rather than confront it. We may think we are trying to protect our friend in this way, but our avoidance implies that he is too weak for our honesty. By seeing him as weak, we unintentionally accentuate his weaknesses; we speak not to him but to the part of him that feels weak. If you are overly tactful because of a friend's perceived weakness, you will both soon feel disconnected, gingerly stepping around the little white lies strewn over the territory of your relationship.

No matter how "tactful" you are, at some level the other person knows what you really mean—just as you know when others are being "tactful" with you. We have all experienced the misery of believing we are so unacceptable that a friend can't be honest with us. This pain leads us to imagine that we suffer from even more serious faults than we actually do.

The opposite of tact is not bluntness that risks inflicting wounds; it is a clear awareness of the real strengths of others. If you are talking on the telephone with a friend and want to return to your work, think of how much you appreciate it when your friend tells you outright when she wishes to hang up, rather than giving you only her divided attention while you talk. Recognizing your friend's strength, you can simply say, "I realize that three-fourths of my mind is on my work. Let's talk more about this later; your ideas are valuable and I want to give them my full attention."

When you have guests who stay too late, you can say to them, "We'd love to be with you longer, but it's our bedtime; we get up very early at our house." If you get to your date's house and he is dressed in cut-offs to dine with you and your favorite aunt, compliment him on his individuality, and tell him what kind of clothes would give you pleasure for this occasion. Look for the humor in your personal preferences, remember to focus on the strength rather than the faults in others, and you will find that tact is rarely needed.

Don't apologize before you speak directly. "I don't know how to tell you this, but I want to be frank with you" are words that make anyone prepare for an attack. Say instead, "I have a strong reaction when you — ——." Then state your reaction, whether it is an impulse to scream, withdraw, feel guilty, get angry. No need to find a reason. You can even say it may be a strange or weird reaction, but a real one. For especially insensitive people, simply state that if you were going to act out your reaction, this is what it would look, feel, and sound like. Then do it.

Children have a natural openness that keeps their friendships close. "I don't want to play now," one says. "OK," says the other, "see you tomorrow." They don't think of making an excuse for not wanting to play, nor do they feel guilty that they don't. They speak and act with an honesty that assumes other people's ability to respond with the same candor.

As "grown-ups" we can add compassion to the honesty we admire in children. We can sustain and even deepen our connections by being aware of the strengths in others before we speak or act. Doing so allows an openness, the kind of openness we have with the friends we respect and enjoy the most.

1. Sit alone by a still body of water or by a large old tree. For as long as possible, recall your forgotten strengths. The more you acknowledge your own strength, the more you will be able to see and appreciate strengths in your friends.
2. Call to mind a friend who speaks openly and honestly without resorting to tact—a friend who stimulates an awareness of your strengths when you are together.
3. The next time you are tempted to overuse tact, think of your honest friend, and remember the good humor you both feel as a result of your openness together. Then, focusing on specific strengths of the person in front of you, speak openly, clearly, and sincerely.

CHAPTER 60

Beyond Attachment: Seeing the Essence Behind the Form

Imagine what would happen if the ocean were to stop taking new forms, if the waves were to freeze just as they stand at a certain moment, as if in a snapshot. The beauty of that moment would endure, but all the future moments would be lost, and so would the special beauty possible only in movement.

When we attach ourselves to anything or anyone, we can become frozen in that moment. No matter how perfect, a frozen moment soon becomes a memory, removed from the flow of life. Joyful relationships thrive on the back-and-forth flow of present moments. The form is always changing. One minute we are a wise teacher, then an eager student, then we put joint ideas into action. If we are attached to relating as a protective parent and our children grow up, we have challenges in relating to them. Forms of relating (being a parent, daughter, teacher, lover) that are no longer alive for us inhibit relationships rather than enhance them.

We also are often tempted to hold others in a frozen form—whether the form is one we like or dislike. (A husband may insist his wife keep her hair long because that's the way it was when they met; a parent may insist on being kissed by a teenager even though the adolescent finds it embarrassing.)

Attachment is often confusing. It can look like love, even be mixed with love. But true love comes from the heart and welcomes any form that is natural and appropriate to its flow of energy. When you love with heart warmth you can allow the form in which your love is expressed to change, knowing that its essence will remain. What delights us at the beach is not a single perfect wave, but the endless interaction of the water, the wind, and the slope of the sand.

In the past, most of us have attached ourselves to experiences of happiness and to those that cause us pain. Both limit us because we become attached to one small experience, of happiness or unhappiness, and cut ourselves off from all the other possibilities.

Likewise, every belief we attach ourselves to limits us. If we believe that scarcity is more probable than abundance in our lives, we soon find scarcity. If we cling to assumptions about what constitutes the ideal relationship, the ideal parent, or even the ideal body, we limit our possibilities. If we attach ourselves to the idea of struggle in a relationship, we make great effort necessary.

As you go through life, growing and changing, you may not always be able to imagine a new form before you give up an old one. Thus you may feel tempted to hold on to what seems real and solid, no matter how it conflicts with your vision. Only by concentrating on what you want rather than on what is dissolving will you bring the new form into focus. Then, like slides simultaneously projected on the same screen, one image will fade out as the next gains shape and clarity.

The new forms that emerge contain more of your life spirit. At any given point in your life you project your current inner picture of yourself —consciously or unconsciously—to create your outside situations. The two will finally match. (Allow for a time lag for the outer situation reflection.) By discovering and cooperating consciously with the new pictures forming inside you, even having the faith that a new picture will form in time, you allow the old pictures to dissolve naturally, and the new outside form to reflect your most radiant self.

Abundance is all around you. When you remember that, it is easier to release attachment to any forms in your life, even familiar ones, that are keeping you in relationships that are no longer alive. Stand ready to marvel at the endless, ever-changing form of communication and interaction that is possible with the special people in your life when you act from the essence of compassion and love. Remember the sublime beauty of the water, the wind, and the slope of the sand.

1. Choose a situation in your life that you suspect may no longer carry a full charge of energy—for example, anything that seems to take a lot of effort.
2. Ask yourself what it represents in your life. At one time the situation expressed an essential value. Look and see whether that value is still present, or whether it has quietly slipped away from the form and no longer enlivens it.
3. Spend a few freewheeling minutes imagining new ways to be with another person that *would* hold energy for you. You will need the poised patience and skill of a butterfly collector to catch these ideas, but the more open you become the more they will come to you in abundance.

CHAPTER 61

Beyond Helping: Empowering Others

The desire to help others comes from your heart. People feel your intention even before you act on it. Your spirit is lifted too. Compassion, whether given or received, raises everyone's spirit.

But if someone demands your help and you consent out of obligation, you both feel weaker—you because you gave in to pressure, and he because he feels dependent on being very needy in order to get a response.

People who feel a need often seek immediate relief rather than trying to fulfill a longer-term desire to be loved, to be financially prosperous, to be powerful, or more effective in their lives. If you attempt to give them immediate relief alone, they are likely to become dependent on you. When you think of someone you want to help, stop and count his or her strengths and innate abilities. Stimulate those strengths. Give this person a vision of his or her own power.

Think of two "needy" people and imagine they don't need your help at all, that they can handle their lives in the best possible way without you. Now see yourself giving them a hand, as you would children jumping over a creek. You would reach out to help them across and then watch them taking off on their adventures together. As they yelled thank you over their shoulders, you would never worry about their dependency on you.

The people who are most determined to get your help will hold up a picture of themselves as helpless, and skillfully lure you into their picture until you believe they really are helpless. If you want to empower them, resist this temptation and instead draw them into your reality. Recognize that the quality that made them so skillful at appearing helpless—their ability to hold a vision and convince others of its reality—is one of their greatest potential assets. Try to help them to select a new vision and convince themselves and others of its reality. Suggest a new vision of success, power, creativity that is just one creek-width-jump away.

Whenever you feel the need to help anyone in any way at all, look deeply within before you take action and see how you can offer a hand while you continue to go about your own work. The other person will know you are acting spontaneously out of your abundance and *belief* in her power to succeed—not grudgingly giving your time, money, or energy—and she will gain new confidence. Your ability to see beyond her temporary needs and to hold that vision clearly will empower her to do the same.

Think of those who have truly helped you to handle your own life more effectively and joyfully. Recall how they encouraged you to clarify exactly where you wanted to go with your life and in some way acknowledged your strength to get there. It's almost as if they could see the path in front of you when you had lost sight of it, and they simply pushed back the underbrush until you found the way again.

The greatest gift you can give others is to invite them to clarify their life's vision, and then support their ability to reach that vision. This leads not to dependency on you, but to the recognition of who they are and how they can present their unique gifts to the world.

1. When you have attempted to give to others what they insisted they "needed" from you, how has your help affected their futures?
2. Think of several people you have helped in the past, without consciously intending to do so. By a few words, sincere listening, a suggestion, or gift of money, you communicated your belief in their ability to reach for success rather than to pull back into a safe harbor.
3. Think of times that someone has empowered you by recognizing your ability. Remember how powerful *you* were after being with this person. Imagine several people in the coming week encouraging you toward your present vision.
4. List a few people, whether you know them personally or not, whom you would enjoy giving a hand to in some way. Do not eliminate people because of the success they *appear* to have. Empower the successful to fulfill their dreams too.

CHAPTER 62

Beyond Anger: Honoring the Deeper Common Purpose

Anger is a powerhouse emotion. It ranges in intensity from annoyance to rage. Whether you explode in anger or let it leak out in sarcasm, "forgetting" commitments, or being late, it gets expressed one way or another.

Anger is not always harmful—to people or relationships. It can help to establish boundaries and make your limits clear. It is a better way to deal with negative emotions than getting sick, lethargic, guilty, or depressed.

Everyone feels anger at some time in a relationship, but not everyone is willing to admit it. We stop our anger any way we can, hiding it not only from our friends or mates, but from ourselves. We think, "What kind of person would get angry over that?" Or, "How foolish I would feel to admit (even to myself) that I have been taken advantage of by this person."

When you acknowledge anger to yourself, you free an enormous amount of energy. The minute you identify the feeling, you release yourself from the impasse of helplessness. Express anger on the spot and it subsides; then you're ready to work on changing the situation. If you hide your anger you will think about it again, and warmed-over anger will turn into resentment.

Anger is a response not to a simple, incontrovertible fact, but to your interpretation of something that has been said or done. Do you believe the other person made an honest (but perhaps stupid) mistake, or that he intended to harm you? The answer to that question is the key to releasing anger.

If you waited for 10 minutes in the rain to meet a friend, you would be angry if you interpreted her lateness as a lack of respect for your time. If you thought she had been in an accident, you would feel worry, not anger. If you knew she was at home frantically preparing a surprise dinner party for you, you would be pleased.

Anger is actually the third step in a build-up of emotion. First is our interpretation of the situation. That stimulates the second step, fear. And the fear leads to anger. A child runs into the street and narrowly misses being hit. His mother's terror quickly turns to anger at the driver. Some-one threatens our security on any level—love, home, work, status, power—and our fears turn into anger. If someone threatened to evict you from your home, would you be angry? It depends. If the person was the little boy who lived next door, you would be indifferent to the threat. But if the threat came from your landlord, you would feel anger and the battle would be on. If your banker threatened eviction after you had missed six months of mortgage payments, you might move from fear, to anger, to guilt or depression.

Unexpressed fear moves quickly into anger, and the cycle repeats itself on increasingly intense levels if you don't interrupt it. All you have to do to stop it is acknowledge, "A wave of fear is sweeping over me." Or, if you miss that step, "A wave of anger is sweeping over me." Wherever you catch the merry-go-round, you can stop it and then look at the fear—most likely it is fear of not being valued fairly.

So long as you refuse to recognize your anger it will keep haunting you. In any relationship you want to keep, don't let yourself hide anger behind a smile or avoid looking directly into the other person's eyes. When you feel anger beginning to build, say that your interpretation of the situation makes you feel angry. Sit down together and honestly express your fears.

If a wave of anger does wash over you, calm your explosive feelings so you can actually hear the other person. If you feel like you can't control the tremendous burst of energy that comes with anger, divert it. Instead of hurling accusations, mop the kitchen floor, clean out the garage, wash the car, yank out weeds in the garden. Keep working hard until the energy is gone, then come back and look objectively at the situation.

The initial expression of anger only takes a minute. Everything after that is "show and tell"—or rather, "blame and guilt." If you hold on to your anger, talking about it over and over, you'll build it to very intense levels. Soon you will have a real fire to put out. (Don't count on any volunteer firemen to help—everyone avoids an angry person.) Accusa-tions made in anger are always exaggerated and can truly hurt others. When you calmly acknowledge a surging feeling of anger, no one is harmed.

Talking about fears calms anger and allows you to connect again with compassion. Acknowledge your real intention to each other. ("I wanted to feel appreciated and valued by you.") Next, talk about your deeper common purpose together. Thus you will learn to understand that—given their fears, hopes, and dreams—the people close to you are doing the very best they can.

Eventually, you will see that the words and actions that used to make you angry are signs of struggle. When your friends, mate, coworkers seem to throw out anger-hooks to you, see them as you would a small child who is struggling to untie a knot in her fishing line, and who has temporarily lost sight (and control) of the end of her line. You would leave her free to master the skill of untying her knot, yet would offer your help if she asked.

All of us are like children untying knots in our lines. We can do it with enthusiasm and fascination—rather than with frustration or anger—once we remember what we are fishing for. We want to connect with something deep—far below the surface—but instead of fish, we can pull in the biggest catch of all—our deeper common purpose.

1. Think about a person you have felt angry with recently.
2. Identify a possible fear about the issue that stimulated your anger.
3. What is your interpretation of the other person's intention—was it to hurt you, or was it an honest (but ignorant or stupid) mistake?
4. Sit down with the other person. Without interruption, explain your fears one at a time. As you feel calmer, talk about your deeper common purpose—together and individually.

CHAPTER 63

Beyond Competition: Cooperating Out of Strength

All of us have days when we don't feel like cooperating with anyone. Instead, we compete for the last word, even with our best friends. If we find another person similarly tempted that day, we are soon engaged in competitive struggles over little things—the best way to cook the omelette or which television program to watch. We even find ourselves competing over who had the hardest day or who is too tired to get the children to bed. The result is usually dismal for both people, and always for one.

When we compete we set ourselves in opposition to someone else; we become like two adversaries in a match. The drive to win may start with a game of tennis or backgammon, but it moves quickly into personal issues. Soon we are competing to be smarter, more capable, more successful. The winner *and* loser inevitably lose, because the competition sabotages the relationship. As the strong gets stronger and the weak gets weaker, both lose all hope of harmonious balance.

We are deeply gratified when someone holds open a door for us to explore more of the rooms in the castle of our own being. They need only to believe in us, to be certain that we have unlimited value, much of which is yet untapped or unexpressed. When we are offered that kind of cooperation, it is easy to release the competitive ways that surround us.

Everyone yearns to be acknowledged as having value. You have a unique opportunity with each person you know, and especially in intimate relationships, to hold up a mirror in which your partner can see his or her value.

We tend to compete in all relationships until we know that we have value by virtue of being loving human beings—we may botch expressing it, but each of us is made up of the substance of love, just as we are made up of the material substance of earth. Knowing this gives us the confidence to delight in bringing out our partner's strength and encouraging her expansion into new territory. The new territory may be building a finer framework for carrying out her life purpose, pursuing greater education, collaborating with new people in her field. She will bring a clearer sense of herself and of her innate value to each of these activities because of our cooperation and support.

You can begin with your own home. Make it a haven where you encourage and are encouraged, where you mirror each other's finest qualities and greatest strengths. In any place you spend time—your office, a restaurant, a grocery store—you can feel the magic of connecting with someone. By genuinely cooperating you can open doors for others to see their innate beauty, strength, power, wisdom, love, compassion.

The more you cooperate, the easier and more natural it becomes, simply because it feels good. Every time you offer cooperation you sense a greater strength within yourself. You quickly become bored with competing with rivals (business and personal) when you see the positive results of reaching out in cooperation.

The more you cooperate, the more people you'll meet who are doing the same, who generously give ideas and expertise, who want you to succeed even though others may think of you as their competitor. Set up ways of receiving and giving cooperation in your business or profession. You can begin today by truly valuing each person's knowledge and talents, rather than competing.

With friends, learn more about cooperation by creating noncompetitive games. (Remember how bad you felt every time you lost at Monopoly or bridge?) Learn synchronized swimming, ballroom dancing, anything that gives both partners great pleasure through cooperating on each movement or step—and which breaks down when competition enters. At home, create games for the family or friends that demand cooperation for any one person to be successful. Everyone will feel closer.

1. Think of one person from your childhood or in your present life by whom you felt appreciated, with whom you felt at peace and in touch with your wholeness and strength. When you think of him or her, notice a specific relaxation in your body.
2. Imagine working on a project with that person, even something as simple as preparing a meal together, and experience in your mind and heart a joyous, productive time together. You are now in touch with the real spirit of cooperation.
3. Now think of a current situation in which you have been tempted to

compete, but in which you would like to create this same spirit of true cooperation. Imagine speaking to the people involved of your intention to cooperate and support the fine work to be done. Suggest ways to do so. Prepare to be surprised by your new spirit of cooperation together the next time you meet.

CHAPTER 64

Beyond Giving or Receiving: Sharing a Joyful Balance

What have you received in your life that has had the most profound effect on you? Which gift was the most precious? Was it a gift of time and energy, of creativity, of money, or something solid that you could hold in your hand?

Many people tell me that of all the gifts they can remember receiving in their lives, they have been most profoundly affected when they received sincere encouragement, when someone believed in them, listened to their dream, and solemnly said, "You can do it. I know you can." Others tell me that when someone offered them a chance to prove themselves—in the third-grade choir, the high school play, the baseball team, their first job, their first official loan—they were given their greatest gifts.

"When someone has accepted me just as I am—with all of my faults." "When a teacher sparked a fire in me to be more than I thought I could be." "When a friend forgave me for making a mistake and then forgot all about it." "When I moved to a new town and my neighbors came over to welcome me." These are the gifts that made a difference in their lives. (All those people received presents at birthdays and at Christmas, yet no one could remember a specific present.)

True giving comes from a heartfelt impulse. An expensive (or inexpensive) gift by itself does not affect us beyond the surface level. A gift given to fill a perceived obligation makes us feel guilty because we cannot summon a wave of enthusiastic appreciation. A gift given so that we will be obligated to the giver makes us think about giving it back. Only the giver's spirit of spontaneous generosity and delight in giving the gift touches our hearts.

All of us know when someone is giving to us from a spirit of compassionate love. And we are always touched by these gifts. Even a wildflower plucked by the hands of a small child and offered to us can be a profound experience in receiving.

Unfortunately, many of us become so intent upon giving to others that we close ourselves off from receiving the kind of gifts that would nourish us. Overly dedicated "givers" attract dedicated "receivers," and it is quite easy to spend your life as a giver, hardly ever receiving. But constant giving, even when our intention in giving is not to win favor or to get anything in return, upsets the natural balance in our relationships.

When you give from a deep desire simply to share, the recipient of your gift receives it with pleasure. Your gift may be a few moments of your time and energy, your creativity, a spontaneous smile, a moment of laughter. Or you may reach out in genuine appreciation of someone you barely know. Encouragement, given with a clear focus, can be a highly significant gift. These are the gifts that can't be packaged and tied up with a ribbon, but are given to the right person at the right time, chosen by your own intuition.

Your most precious gift is your spirit of joy. That is the gift that allows others to see a greater vision of who they are. (Giving a beautiful flower, vase, book, candle with your joy is an extra.) All of us feel a simple pleasure in knowing another joyful person—and of acknowledging together the generosity of the universe. Joy is free. Anyone can have it, anyone can give it.

The more you give in this spirit, the more you receive of true value. And the more you expand your range of people who give to you and also are willing to receive from you, the more you strike a joyful balance. At a certain point you will discover that you can no longer discern who is giving and who is receiving. It may feel as if you receive continuously, regardless of how many ways you give to others.

Having experienced the exultation of giving—and receiving—for the pure pleasure of each interaction, who would do otherwise?

1. Think of a few heartfelt gifts you joyfully gave to others recently— even if you didn't realize at the time that you were "giving" anything —and recall the feeling as you gave them.
2. Now remember the feeling you had as they were received in the same spirit of joy.
3. Recall a recent time when you wholeheartedly accepted a gift from someone, friend or stranger, whether a smile, a word of encouragement, or a gift placed in your hands. Remember how you felt at that moment. Surprised? Delighted? Appreciated?
4. Compare both feelings about yourself—when your gift was accepted and when you gratefully received a gift. When both occasions feel equally fulfilling, you will know you are ready to share a joyful balance of giving and receiving.

A Personal Message from the Author

This book is not an idealistic, misty-eyed dream. Every chapter holds a clear vision that can draw you toward a more rewarding and fulfilling pattern of relating to anyone—from the newsstand proprietor to the people closest to you. Each time you experiment with the suggested steps you will reactivate the finest qualities you have gained from all your past experiences, and free them to contribute to your relationships now.

In reading this book you have reached within to see more of who you are, to get a sense of your own purpose in life. You are the creator of your future. You can decide to walk a path of joy with all the people you know —and many you will meet. By using the chapters and cards as an *ongoing* guide, you will discover your own power to truly enjoy your life. Clarity, truth, love, and wisdom are waiting within you to enrich your relationships with others and with your self.

As you practice relating to people from new perspectives, remember that the changes in your relationships often will not show on the surface until the new underlying structures have time to take shape. The first blossoms of spring appear overnight only because the plants have been steadily growing under the ground.

None of us can apply all sixty-four ways of connecting to every relationship every day. Concentrate on the moments in which you reach for new patterns, and those occasions will multiply week by week. Soon you will find your life filled with expressions of love, understanding, and encouragement—both given and received.

As you share your stories and your cards with your friends, perhaps you will inspire them to discover their own paths of joy, compassion, shared wisdom, and purpose. I would enjoy hearing from you as you have new experiences of connecting that enrich your life or the lives of others.

LaUna Huffines

LaUna Huffines
Box 5019
Mill Valley, California 94942